D1556087

BAVARIA

(*Frontispiece, overleaf*) 1 *The Badenburg, in the grounds of the Schloss Nymphenburg, near Munich*

James Bunting

BAVARIA

B. T. Batsford Ltd London

First published 1972

© James Bunting 1972

Text printed in Great Britain by Northumberland Press Ltd.,
Gateshead. Plates printed and books bound by Richard Clay
(The Chaucer Press) Ltd., Bungay, Suffolk

ISBN 0 7134 0167 2

For Carola and Toni Koch with love

Contents

The Plates

10 *The Plates*

Acknowledgments

I must express my gratitude to the *Fremdenverkehrsverbände* in Munich, Nürnberg, Regensburg and Füssen for their advice and assistance, and also to the ever helpful German Tourist Information Bureau in London. I wish specially to thank Dr Hans Sigmund, Dr Karl Koch, Ludwig Müller and Paula Horst for supplying me with various items of information, and my wife, Trudi, for translating some of Adalbert Stifter's writings and generally helping me out with my German.

The author and the publishers wish to thank the following for supplying photographs reproduced in this book: J. Allan Cash for plate 4; and A. F. Kersting for plates 1-3, 5-7, 10, 14, 15, 17-19, and 21-23.

1. Introduction

Bavaria is by far the largest of all the German states or *Länder*, its area being nearly a third of that of the whole Federal Republic. For more than seven centuries it was a separate monarchy, being ruled by members of the house of Wittelsbach, first as dukes, then as electors and finally as kings. And, although it became a republican state in 1918, it still retains much of its old autonomy. Its inhabitants are intensely proud of their native land. They regard themselves as being set apart from the other German peoples and they are inclined to look upon their ancient capital, Munich, as being the first city of the Republic.

It has often been said that, so far as its topography and native characteristics are concerned, Germany closely resembles Great Britain turned upside down. Bavaria certainly supports this contention. It lies in the extreme south-east of the Republic, yet its people exhibit all the warmth, generosity and hospitality shown by the people of the Western Highlands of Scotland. Nor does the similarity stop there, for the south of Bavaria, with its lakes, mountains and forests, remind one vividly of Inverness-shire, whilst the north resembles the Border Counties. And Munich will be found curiously reminiscent of Edinburgh.

The Bavarians are extremely devout. Nearly three-quarters of the country's ten million population are Roman Catholics, most of the remainder being Protestants, and there are very few of either persuasion who are not regular churchgoers. On Sunday mornings, the town streets, the hills and the valleys echo and re-echo with the sound of countless deep, melodious church bells.

I first visited Bavaria as a small boy and was so deeply impressed that, for months afterwards, I could talk of nothing else. The country had seemed to me like some fabulous dreamland, with its fantastic castles, blue lakes, dense pine forests and snow-capped peaks. I did not return until ten years later – having spent some of the intervening time in Switzerland and Italy – and I fully expected to have my childhood memories and illusions shattered. But no. I still found myself gaping unashamedly at the height of the Ulm cathedral spire, at the monstrous baroque splendour of Neuschwanstein, at the stark beauty of the Bavarian Alps, at the mysterious, mountain-locked waters of the Königsee, at the magnificence of Munich.

Therein lies the whole secret of Bavaria's fascination. You can go back again and again as I have, you can even stay each time at the same place, and still the scenery never palls. And around almost every bend in the road you will discover some new marvel of architecture, some breathtaking change of landscape. I know of no other place in the world that can produce the same effect.

Besides its natural attractions, Bavaria offers its visitors so many unique local diversions that it is virtually impossible to cover them all in the space of a lifetime. There are the Mozart Summer Festival at Augsburg, the Children's Pageant at Dinkelsbühl, the Dance Festival at Kaufbeuren, the St George's Day Ride at Traunstein, the Vintner's Festival at Würzburg, the Toy Fair at Nürnberg, the Shepherds' Dancing at Rothenburg, the Oktoberfest at Munich and the Memingen Fishermen's Day, just to mention a few. And, of course, every ten years, Oberammergau presents its world-famous and unforgettable Passion Play. Generally speaking, there is not a single Bavarian town, large or small, that does not stage a show of some sort at least once a year. And most of the villages have their own individual carnivals.

Bavaria also caters sumptuously for the inner man. It is not, as some people may have been led to believe, a land where they eat nothing but sausage and drink nothing but lager. The Bavarians are rightly proud of their culinary versatility and even the smallest *gasthaus* or *weinstube* will dish you up a meal fit for a king at a price to suit the pocket of the humblest courtier. Moreover, although the Bavarian beers are frequently claimed to be the best in the world, there is a wide selection of extremely palatable local wines.

Do not be deterred from visiting Bavaria if you cannot speak or understand German. English is part of the curriculum in all Bavarian schools and there are no towns and very few villages where it is not spoken to at least a small degree by the inhabitants. The Bavarians also, unlike some other Continentals, delight in airing their knowledge of the language and will bend over backwards to do so. You can also take heart in the fact that the countrymen speak German with such a thick accent that often their own compatriots find them practically unintelligible!

If you happen to be motoring in Bavaria, you will find that the roads are so well signposted that it is impossible to get lost. And, if you should find yourself completely stuck, there are information offices (*Verkehrsbüros*) or travel offices (*Reisebüros*) in almost every town, where English is spoken fluently.

Some British people might be detracted from going to Bavaria on the grounds that it is too far away. Yet the flight from London to Munich takes less than two hours and costs only a pound or two more than the flight from London to Geneva. Admittedly it is a two days' drive for the motorist, but personally I always pick up a self-drive hire car when I get to Munich or, for that matter, to Stuttgart. The rates are about 15 per cent less than in England and you have nothing else to pay, apart from the fuel. What's more, you are saved the long drive back home, which often puts paid to the benefits you have received from your holiday.

As for the Bavarian climate, it is very similar to that obtaining in the extreme south of England, except that it is a little warmer in summer and a little colder in winter. On an average, the rainfall in summer is considerably less than it is in the British Isles, but the winter snowfall is much heavier, especially in the Alpine regions. You must not expect to get as sunburnt in Bavaria as you will in the Mediterranean, but you will acquire a healthy tan. The natives themselves are evidence of this.

To understand Bavaria and the Bavarians more thoroughly, it is necessary to know something about the country's historical background. It will then be seen how the trials and tribulations of more than 15 centuries have moulded the character of the people, shaped their destiny and added to their heritage.

The earliest inhabitants of Bavaria were most probably Celts, although nothing of significance has been found to suggest that they existed in large numbers and, whoever they might have been, they were quickly driven out when the Romans first invaded the territory in 15 B.C. In time the country became part of the Roman province of Rhaetia and, later, the famous Rhaetian *limes* – or fortified border line – was constructed over the 200 kilometres that lay between Regensburg and Lorch, in northern Austria. A Roman legion was stationed at Regensburg, then known as Castra Regina, and another camp was established on the site of Augsburg.

In spite of this, very little in the way of Roman remains has been discovered elsewhere in Bavaria. The country was mostly used for purposes of transit and probably not more than 2,000 or 3,000 Romans occupied it at any one time. This undoubtedly explains why only a feeble resistance was offered when the barbarian Alemanni and Juthungi overran the territory in the early part of the fifth century, driving south the remnants of the Roman militia.

2   *Obermarchtal, near Ulm: the Abbey Church, seen from the Danube*

The barbarians were not left unharassed for long. They were quickly subdued by the Franks, who were then steadily extending their empire into southern Germany. The first-known ruler of Bavaria – of Roman descent and titled Duke Garibaldi I – acknowledged Frankish sovereignty in A.D. 550 and, shortly afterwards, succeeded in gaining a degree of independence for his country. By all accounts, Garibaldi was a cantankerous, quarrelsome character and this led to a series of violent squabbles amongst rival claimants to rulership, which lasted for over 150 years and finally resulted in the Franks intervening. The Frankish king, Charles Martel – grandfather of Charlemagne and known as the 'Hammer' – stepped in and became supreme overlord in 730. In 763, 22 years after the death of Charles Martel, Bavaria regained its independence under the rulership of Duke Tassilo III, who was ultimately forced to recognise the sovereignty of Charlemagne in 781 and was deposed seven years later. Bavaria was added to the Carolingian Empire and became officially a part of the eastern Frankish kingdom with the signing of the Treaty of Verdun in 843. In the meantime, the Bavarian people had become Christians, thanks to the efforts of some itinerant Roman monks who had set up headquarters in Augsburg and had been quietly establishing monasteries and churches whilst the pagan rulers had been engaged elsewhere.

With the Carolingian Empire beginning to crack up early in the tenth century, Bavaria once again reverted to local rulership. A number of self-styled dukes appeared upon the scenes who, when not engaged in fighting off the constantly invading Magyars, quarrelled tempestuously amongst themselves. For a while the descendants of Luitpold, margrave of Ostmark (Austria), held sway, but they were ousted by Henry, brother of Otto the Great, King of the Germans, in 948, and for a while Bavaria became part of the German kingdom. Finally, towards the end of the eleventh century, Henry IV of

3 Dinkelsbühl: one of the gateways to the old town

Germany presented the duchy to Count Welf of Swabia, a forerunner of the Guelph family.

The Guelphs retained Bavaria not without considerable difficulty for 80 years, when Count Welf's grandson, Duke Henry the Proud, lost it to Leopold of Babenberg, another margrave of Ostmark. His successor and brother, Henry Jasomirgott, then ceded Bavaria to his nephew Henry the Lion in 1156, who was finally deposed by the Bavarian Count Otto of Wittelsbach in 1180.

Thus began the great dynasty of the Wittelsbachs, unbroken for 738 years. However, although they brought considerable prosperity to the Bavarian people, they were unable to prevent the duchy from shrinking in size and power. During the thirteenth century, many wealthy landowners, some of whom were important ecclesiastical dignitaries, decided to break away from Bavaria and turn their holdings into independent states. This resulted in the founding of the borderland counties of Schaumburg and Tirol and the bishoprics of Eichstätt, Freising, Passau, Regensburg and Salzburg. What was left of Bavaria was mainly contained between the rivers Lech, Danube and Inn.

This breakaway was further complicated by alterations to the internal structure of Bavaria itself. When Otto II, grandson of the first Otto, died in 1253, his two sons decided to divide the country more or less equally between them – into Upper Bavaria and Lower Bavaria. A few years later, their own sons further split the territory into six. The mind boggles at what would have happened if matters had been allowed to continue in this fashion; one has terrifying visions of a thousand Wittelsbachs each ruling over a domain not much larger than Brighton or Blackpool! But mercifully the divisions gave rise to a whole series of family squabbles and, after a bickering that lasted for some 250 years (the Bavarians were nothing if not long-winded in their arguments!), the duchy took its first step towards unity. Albert, Duke of Munich, commandeered the provinces of Landshut and Ingolstadt, whilst the principalities of Neuburg and Sulzbach were given to the two sons of Rupert, Count Palatine.

Albert certainly deserved his subsequent appellation of 'the Wise'. In 1506, he introduced the law of primogeniture, aimed at securing the succession and preventing any further division of territory. Even so, there were further squabbles between his two sons after his death and it was not until after the younger son, Louis, died in circumstances that do not bear close investigation in the year 1545, that the elder son, Duke William IV, succeeded in uniting Bavaria completely. William IV was an ardent Catholic and it was largely due to his firm resistance to the Protestant movement, then sweeping all Europe, that Bavaria has remained strongly Roman Catholic to this day. His successors Albert V (1550-79) and William V (1579-97) fought Protestant 'heresy' tooth and nail and Duke Maximilian I, who followed in 1597, founded the Catholic League in 1609. He was a wise, strong and much-loved ruler who, when he died in 1651, left Bavaria a thriving country, despite a series of disastrous wars with the Swedes and the French. What was even more important, he established Bavaria as an Electorate, second only to the Habsburg State, which meant that it now had a right in the election of an emperor of all Germany.

Following the death of Maximilian I, Bavaria settled down to what looked as if it might be a steady, peaceful existence. France and Austria were at loggerheads with each other, but the Bavarians managed to keep out of the dispute by maintaining an elaborate and well-thought-out turncoat policy, siding first with one country and next with the other. But at the turn of the century Maximilian I's grandson, Maximilian Emmanuel, committed a serious blunder by taking sides with the French against Austria in the War of the Spanish Succession. His army suffered severe defeat at Blenheim in 1704 and his country was confiscated. It was ultimately restored to him ten years later by the Treaty of Rastatt, but it was in such a sorry state that it seemed as if it would never again become of any significance. And it was still very largely under the domination of the Austrians.

With Charles Albert becoming Elector in 1726, Bavaria slowly improved its economy, only to run into fresh trouble following the death of the Emperor Charles VI in 1740. Charles had abandoned his claim to the throne of Spain by the Treaty of Utrecht in 1714 and had spent the remainder of his days in securing succession to the Austrian throne for his daughter Maria Theresa. But now Charles Albert of Bavaria stepped in and claimed Austria and all the Habsburg possessions for himself. He presented himself as the rightful heir on the rather shaky authority that his kinsman Maximilian Emmanuel had married Maria Antonia, sister of the Habsburg Charles II of Spain.

Thus began the War of the Austrian Succession. For a while, it ran all in Bavaria's favour. Charles Albert was proclaimed King of Bohemia and was elected Emperor of Austria in January 1742. Then, on the very day that he was to be crowned, Munich was captured by the Austrians. They proceeded to hold Bavaria for more than two years, when it was finally restored to the much humbled and greatly subservient Charles Albert. He died shortly afterwards, on 20 January 1745, leaving his eight-year-old son, Maximilian Joseph, as his successor.

Wise counsellors now decided that the only way to save Bavaria from oblivion was to make peace with the Austrians once and for all. Maximilian Joseph was advised to renounce all claim to the throne of Austria and his possessions were later restored to him by means of Pragmatic Sanction. This was a solemn decree by which his powers as a sovereign were categorically and inexorably defined. The term *pragmatica sanctio* originated in Roman Law and has now become obsolete.

There can be no doubt that this course marked a turning point in Bavarian history. Relinquishing all pretensions to power politics, Maximilian Joseph concentrated his efforts on restoring his country's erstwhile prosperity. Agriculture became a major activity of the Bavarians, swords were beaten into ploughshares and, in the big towns, there was a great revival in learning and the arts.

Maximilian was at a complete loss to know what to do original Bavarian branch of the Wittelsbach family became extinct. But there were still Wittelsbachs in other parts of Germany and the Electorate went to Charles Theodore, ruler of the Sulzbach and Rhenish Palatinates. He came as a complete stranger to Bavaria and what he saw obviously did not please him, because he immediately opened negotiations for the sale or exchange of his new domain. This move was fortunately frustrated by Frederick II of Prussia and so, once again, Bavaria was saved from annihilation by absorption. Charles Theodore was forced to carry on as Elector and promptly proceeded to imperil his possessions by joining the first anti-French coalition at the outbreak of the French Revolution. He was ill-advised in his choice of alliance and, for a while, French troops occupied Bavaria and also his Rhenish Palatinate.

Charles Theodore died without issue in 1799 and Bavaria passed into the hands of the Birkenfeld Wittelsbachs. From them sprang the next Elector, Maximilian Joseph II, who became the first King of Bavaria (Maximilian I) in 1806.

Maximilian was at a complete loss to know what to do regarding the French and had he not had the able assistance of one of the greatest government ministers in Bavarian history, Count Maximilian Montgelas, it seems likely that Bavaria would have become part of the Napoleonic Empire, at least for a time. As it was, he was forced to cede the territories which had been annexed by the French and, after placing himself under French protection in 1801, he had to exchange the Bavarian outer dependencies for the collection of bishoprics which had sprung up in the thirteenth century. As some compensation, he gained some additional ground by the Treaty of Pressburg in 1805, including the Austrian provinces of Tirol and Vorarlberg.

After proclaiming himself king, Maximilian continued to side with the French and, although he lost part of the Tirol at the peace of Schönbrun in 1809, he gained more valuable territories, including the abbey of Berchtesgaden and the principality of Regensburg. Finally, in 1813, he saw which way the wind was blowing and joined with Germany against Napoleon. This shrewd move resulted in Bavaria becoming the third largest and most important German state, next to Prussia and Austria.

Maximilian was succeeded in 1825 by his 40-year-old son, Ludwig I. At first a wise and able ruler, albeit an artist and an eccentric, Ludwig slowly turned into a rebellious reactionary, despised by his ministers for his loose morals and hated by his people for the crippling taxes which he enforced upon them. Matters came to a head in 1846, when he formed an association with the adventuress and self-styled Spanish dancer, Lola Montez (of whom more will be related in another chapter). As his mistress and created by him Countess of Landsfeld, she dominated the political scene for nearly two years and drew large sums from the Bavarian treasury, resulting in even more taxation being imposed. Finally the people of Bavaria revolted – something which was entirely against their nature – and Ludwig I was forced to abdicate in 1848.

Now Maximilian II, Ludwig's son, came to the throne and speedily involved his country in yet another struggle for power, this time between Austria and Prussia. Again Bavaria backed the wrong horse and, as a result, was compelled to pay a war indemnity of 30 million gulden to Prussia and to hand over part of South Franconia.

The reign of Maximilian II will be best remembered for the activities of the Catholic theologian, Johann Joseph Ignaz von Döllinger, who was born in Bamberg, Bavaria, in 1799 and who was appointed to the chair of ecclesiastical history and law at Munich University in 1826. A violent anti-Protestant and staunch upholder of the Catholic faith, von Döllinger modified his views after a visit to Rome in 1857. Thereafter he shook the whole Christian world by stating that the progress of the Roman Catholic Church did not depend upon the sovereignty of the Pope and, later, he assailed the whole dogma of papal infallibility. He was excommunicated in 1871 and expelled from the university two years afterwards. He spent his latter days in trying to organise a union of Christian Churches not belonging to the Roman Communion. He died without seeing his vision fulfilled.

Maximilian II died in 1864 and the throne passed to his son, Ludwig II. This unhappy young man, only 21 at the time of his succession, was responsible for what must be undoubtedly the saddest chapter in the history of the Bavarian monarchy. An acknowledged homosexual and an ardent lover of music, he spent vast sums of money on extravagant theatrical projects put forward by his protégé, Richard Wagner, most of which were utterly impracticable. At the same time, he became afflicted by a tragic mental illness which grew steadily worse and he was declared unfit to rule in 1886. After this, he was virtually held prisoner for a short while in the Castle of Starnberg and committed suicide there by throwing himself into the lake, dragging his handcuffed attendant with him.

Ludwig's brother Otto was next in line to the throne and he also was insane. Otto theoretically ruled Bavaria for 27 years, but the monarchy was actually in the hands of two successive Regents. The first of these, Prince Luitpold, uncle of Ludwig II and Otto, took over the Regency three days before the former's suicide. He was succeeded by his son – another Ludwig – in 1912, who became King Ludwig III on the death of Otto on 5 November 1913.

Five years later, almost to the day, the long Wittelsbach dynasty came to an end. After a protest meeting against the continuance of the First World War, the Bavarian Socialists set up a government under the German-Jewish statesman, Kurt Eisner, on 8 November 1918. On the 13th, Ludwig III was forced to abdicate. But the revolutionary régime was short-lived. Eisner was assassinated on 21 February 1919, and a coalition government was then formed with the Majority Socialist, Hoffmann, as minister-president. He was quickly deposed by a Bolshevik uprising and on 4 April Bavaria was proclaimed a Communist Soviet Republic, with Ernst Toller, Levine and Landauer in command.

But Hoffmann was determined not to take this lying down. Supported by remnants of the Prussian army, he besieged Munich and starved it into surrendering on 1 May. The Hoffmann government was restored on 5 May, Toller was imprisoned, Levine court-martialled and shot and Landauer murdered. Bavaria now returned to comparative sanity and later adopted a right-wing political policy. Hoffmann was succeeded by von Kahr as minister-president, who was ousted by Count Lerchenfeld who, in turn, was replaced by von Knilling.

It was then that the first Bavarian Nationalist movement was started by von Kahr, the Reich military dictator General von Lossow and Colonel Seisser, chief of police. It showed some signs of succeeding and might well have done so had it not been compelled to alter its plans by the sudden rise of Adolf Hitler, who was organising a similar movement of his own. Hitler endeavoured to get von Kahr and von Lossow to join him but they let him down. Hitler's plan to march on Berlin then failed, as did also his attempt to overthrow the Bavarian government, and von Kahr remained a disappointed man for the rest of his days. General von Seekt was appointed by the Reich to maintain order in Bavaria and he subsequently signed a deed of agreement with von Knilling (the Peace of Homburg). The latter resigned shortly afterwards and Dr Held became head of the next coalition.

Dr Held spent most of his political career in asserting the rights of Bavaria as a free country within the German Federation, but his efforts were nipped in the bud when Hitler came into power and merged Bavaria with the Third Reich.

Although the National Socialist movement was born in Munich, the Bavarians never looked upon it kindly. They also disliked and distrusted the Führer. He was to them always an Austrian and Austrians had been responsible for more than half of their country's past troubles. Even in Berchtesgaden – where Hitler had his favourite holiday residence, later to become a war headquarters – the townspeople pointedly stayed indoors when he drove through the streets in his bullet-proof Mercedes. And, when hostilities commenced, many of the peasantry succeeded in avoiding military service, not because they were frightened of being killed – no Bavarian could ever be accused of that – but because they were morally and spiritually opposed to warfare.

I was in the Allgäu in the early summer of 1939 and I was frankly amazed by the atmosphere of gloomy foreboding that pervaded the whole area. It was in such direct contrast to the boisterous *sieg heilings* of those in other parts of the Reich. I was also deeply moved by the great kindness that was shown to me, an Englishman whom they knew was destined very shortly to become an enemy.

But that is all part of the Bavarian character. A character that has been moulded by the historical events I have just described. The Bavarians have seen abject poverty and they have known great prosperity. They have been subjugated in bitter defeat and they have risen high on the wave of glorious victory. Their native land has probably been subjected to more partitioning, more intrigue, more internal quarrelling, more chopping and changing than any other country in Europe. But they have always had the courage to rise above vicissitudes, even when Augsburg, Munich and other Bavarian cities were the victims of a heavy and continuous bombardment in the Second World War such as England never had to bear. And they have never lost their faith in God and in humanity.

The Bavarian outlook is typified by the blue and white sign that greets all those who cross its frontiers by road. Bearing the Wittelsbach coat of arms it reads 'Freistaat Bayern' – the Free State of Bavaria. A free people with a noble heritage. A free country that, as you will discover when you read on, is rich in tradition, in scenic splendour, in architecture, in learning and in the arts.

2. Swabia: Ulm and Augsburg

Had you been in the city of Ulm on a certain summer's day in 1811, you would have been able to witness one of man's earliest attempts to fly. It was the occasion of the King of Württemberg's state visit and, by way of a tribute, a loyal but somewhat impecunious little tailor named Albrecht Ludwig Berblinger decided to soar above the Danube on a pair of large and cumbersome home-made wings attached to his arms. Watched by more than half the town's population, he leapt from the top of Ulm's fortified ramparts and, a few seconds later, plunged straight into the river. Fortunately he survived the ordeal, but it put an end to his aviation ambitions and, shortly afterwards, his wife sold the remains of his wings to a local umbrella maker!

More than a century later, in 1916, another native of Ulm, Albert Einstein, made scientific history by publishing his theory of relativity. But this time the population remained singularly unmoved. For one thing, they were busily engaged in making munitions for their compatriots on the Western Front and had little time for what was going on in the outside world. For another, there were few who remembered that Einstein had been born in their midst only 37 years before. It was in the narrow streets just east of the Minster that the young Albert had played as a small boy, before being taken to Munich to begin his education, and people who lived in that area kept themselves very much to themselves. However, whilst visiting Ulm in the early 30s, I did meet one old couple who remembered Einstein as a child. They described him as being very shy and backward and were frankly amazed that he had grown up to be one of the greatest mathematical geniuses of the century.

Ulm is frequently described as the main gateway to Bavaria, although the old town, situated on the north bank of the Danube, lies just within the boundary of Württemberg, to which state it was ceded in 1809. But the majority of its inhabitants like to be regarded as Bavarians and, in any case, the modern town of Neu-Ulm, on the opposite side of the river, is undeniably a part of the Freistat. So I feel there is ample justification for including Ulm in this chapter, particularly as it played a decisive part in Bavaria's more recent history. It was, in fact, the scene of one of Napoleon's speediest victories.

At the end of September 1805 the spearhead of Napoleon's army – including detachments commanded by Soult and Ney – had crossed the Rhine and was pressing forwards to the Danube at the then almost incredible rate of 30 miles a day. On 6 October the French encountered some 45,000 Austrians and Bavarians – under Schwarzenburg, Reisch and Warneck – raised against them in the Ulm area. By the 9th the Archduke Ferdinand had brought his men closer in and had encircled Ulm with defending troops. Five days later, the Austrian commander Mack, with 27,000 men, became almost completely surrounded at Ulm by nearly three times the number of French. Napoleon demanded his immediate surrender, but Mack continued to hold out until the 20th, by which time his generals had mutinied and had started to negotiate their own peace treaty. The whole campaign against Ulm had lasted no more than a fortnight and it had been a comparatively bloodless siege, with 50 Austrians and Bavarians being captured to each one killed. But it had paved Napoleon's way to Munich and Innsbruck and was the curtain-raiser to the Austerlitz campaign.

During the early part of the twentieth century, Ulm became an important railway junction, with the third largest marshalling yard in Germany. This naturally made it a target for the

Allied bombers in the Second World War but, fortunately, the yard was situated some distance to the north of the old town, so that most of its historical buildings survived extensive damage and some of them remained virtually unscathed.

Dominating the whole town and visible for miles around is the massive Cathedral Minster, the second largest Gothic church in Germany, being only slightly smaller than the one in Cologne. The original building dates from 1377 and considerable additions were made in the two centuries following, although construction work of one kind or another proceeded sporadically right up to the end of the nineteenth century.

Perhaps the cathedral's greatest claim to fame is its immense spire, which was completed in 1890 in accordance with the original designs of Matthäus Böblinger, who built the ancient tower upon which it stands. Rising to the height of 161 metres (528 feet), it is the loftiest church spire in the world. As a young man, I once climbed the 768 steps leading to within a short distance of the spire's summit, but I would never do it again and I do not recommend the exercise to anyone who is not sound in wind and limb and who cannot stand heights. Nevertheless, the view from the top is extremely rewarding in fine weather, including a truly stupendous panorama of Lake Constance, with all the Swiss Alps spread out beyond. I have heard it alleged that, given a suitably powered telescope, it is even possible to see the coastline of England on an exceptionally clear day, but I have never met anyone who has done so. However, technically-minded people with a knowledge of contours and the earth's curvature have told me that it is not beyond the bounds of credibility.

The interior of the Minster, as one might expect from its outward appearance, is most awe-inspiring. There are five naves, the main one rising to a height of nearly 100 feet, mostly the work of Bukhardt Engelberg, and the massive, strong pillars supporting the roof are embellished with Swabian sculptures that have withstood the test of time wonderfully well. Even more spectacular are the magnificent choir stalls, carved by the master-craftsman Jörg Syrlin the Elder round about the year 1470. They are larger and richer in figurework than any other choir stalls in Germany and I would draw attention especially to the fine head of a priest, which is undoubtedly one of the world's wood carving masterpieces. I have seen many such works of art during my lifetime and I would couple this priest's head with the carving of Christ in Konstanz Cathedral as the finest of them all.

Rising above the choir stalls is the high altar by Martin Schaffner, another outstanding example of medieval craftsmanship, surmounted by the tall and slender east windows with their highly valuable glass paintings by Hans Acker and Peter von Andlau.

The last time I visited Ulm Cathedral there was an organ recital in progress and I cannot too strongly recommend any lover of music to try and enjoy the same experience. This should not prove too difficult, because such recitals are fairly frequent and, if I recollect rightly, there is a notice just inside the main entrance which lists the dates and times of day. The organ has 95 stops and 8,000 pipes and the acoustics of the Cathedral, whether by accident or design, are as near perfect as can be, so that the whole building becomes alive with beautiful harmony. Every time I hear Bach's Toccata and Fugue I am reminded of the old Minster at Ulm, and I have never heard it rendered more magnificently, either before or since.

Very conveniently situated in the Münsterplatz close to the main entrance to the Cathedral is Ulm's information bureau, where English visitors are made particularly welcome and can learn all they want to know about the town and about the accommodation it offers. I feel I should stress at this point that all the information offices in Bavaria are of a very high standard indeed and are staffed by English-speaking men and women, augmented by bright young students in the summer season, who will bend over backwards to be helpful.

Many of Ulm's most ancient and historic buildings also lie within a stone's throw of the Cathedral and, curiously enough, they seem to fit in perfectly with the modern shopping centres that flank them. The old Rathaus (Town Hall), 200 yards south of the Münsterplatz, must certainly be seen. It was originally built as a market in 1370, became the Rathaus 50 years later and is a mixture of late Gothic and Renaissance architecture, with fine painted frescoes on the walls. On the south gable is a representation of Ulm's coat of arms, composed of the arms of those places with which the town did extensive trade during the Middle Ages, and there is an interesting astronomical clock on the east gable. The Town Hall was one of the places that did suffer war damage, being bombed in 1944, but it has been restored with loving care to its original splendour.

Just south of the Rathaus is the Metzgerturm (Butcher's Tower), which was built in 1340. It is proudly described as Ulm's own 'leaning tower', its summit being 2·05 metres (6½ feet) out of vertical and inclined towards the north-west.

A minute's walk eastwards from the Town Hall will bring you to the Museum, which is established in three old manor houses complete with dovecotes. It contains a representative collection of arts and crafts from Ulm and Swabia, from which a lot may be learnt about life and activity in the district. If you now go north, leaving the Cathedral on your left, you will come to the Kornhaus (Corn Exchange), first built in 1407, renovated in the sixteenth century and gutted by fire in 1944. It now houses a modern concert hall.

No visitor should ever leave Ulm without taking a stroll along the Danube waterfront, because here will be found a truly Gothic ambience, so calm and peaceful that it immediately transports you back to medieval times. The ancient, crooked houses, many of them built right on the water's edge, are clustered together in groups, along with their churches, and are separated at intervals by narrow streets and cobbled squares in some of which are fountains. The district is easiest reached by walking down the short Donaustrasse, just east of the Museum. At the bottom of this, on the left, is the Reichnauerhof, a fine example of an old manor house, with its commemorative plaque and ornate ceremonial hall. Ulm used to abound with such buildings in the Middle Ages; they were the homes of the wealthy *patrizieren*, the town's commercial aristocracy.

I have already stated that Bavaria is rich in festivals and pageantry and if you travel 52 kilometres (33 miles) south from Ulm and the month happens to be July, you will be able to experience one of these historic folklore events. This is Fishermen's Day – in reality the best part of a week – when all the 40,000 inhabitants of Memmingen appear, to the Englishman's eye at any rate, to go completely berserk. There is dancing in the streets and vast quantities of beer and wine are consumed by all and sundry. One of the more lovable things about the Germans, and especially the Bavarians, is that they do take their fun very seriously.

Even if you miss Fishermen's Day, Memmingen is still worth a brief visit. It has an interesting fifteenth-century church, St Martin's, with choir stalls by Hans Herlin and Heinrich Stark (1501-8) that, in some respects, can almost be said to rival those in Ulm. And in the Church of Our Lady you will find some splendid frescoes, the work of the Strigel family in 1470. There is also a late sixteenth-century house that once belonged to the Fuggers, a family of whom we shall learn a lot more when we come to Augsburg.

About 45 kilometres (28 miles) east of Memmingen lies the picturesque old town of Landsberg, on the river Lech. Here they also have their own particular form of junketing – the Ruethenfest – but, since it takes place only once in every five years, not many visitors are able to enjoy it. Landsberg is a very well-preserved example of medievalism, with its quaint square surrounded by towers and fortifications, and has a fine fourteenth-century parish church, converted to baroque in the seventeenth century. It was in the fortress here that Hitler was once imprisoned and wrote his celebrated *Mein Kampf*, although the people of Landsberg no longer boast about it. The fine eighteenth-century Johanneskirche and Ursulinenkirche are the works of that great master of rococo, Dominikus Zimmermann, who lies buried in Wies, not far from Füssen.

The road leading north from Landsberg to Augsburg follows close to the river and traverses the historic Lechfeld, where one of the bloodiest battles in Bavarian history was fought more than 1,000 years ago. It was here, in 955, that Otto the Great inflicted a crushing defeat on the raiding Magyars and stopped their incursions forever, driving them back to settle permanently in the country that later became Hungary. In the nearby villages, some of the old people will tell you that, on dark, misty nights at certain times of the year, you can hear the battle being fought all over again by ghost armies. At such times the inhabitants bolt their doors and remain breathlessly behind barred shutters, but they don't seem any the worse for the experience and I doubt whether the legend will persist much further in this modern, matter-of-fact age!

When approaching Augsburg, either by road or by rail, do not be discouraged by its rather depressing industrial environs. It is less than a quarter of the size of Munich, but it is now the largest manufacturing district in Bavaria and, indeed, has been a centre of commerce ever since the Middle Ages, when it lay on the main trade route from Germany to Italy and the Mediterranean. But the old town itself is a delight to behold and, once you have arrived at the spectacular Rotes Tor (Red Gate), the main entrance from the south, you will realise that you are heading for something very special.

The town dates back to the early days of Roman occupation and takes its name from the Emperor Augustus, to whose memory a magnificent fountain has been erected in the town centre. A few hundred yards to the north of this, at the top of the Hoher Weg, is the High Cathedral, founded in A.D. 923 and see of the Roman Catholic bishop. The building began its life as an early Christian baptismal church (some of the walls of which may still be seen) and was later reconstructed to a romanesque design and Gothicised in 1396-1431. The two tall spires were added towards the end of the fifteenth century.

One of the most interesting of the High Cathedral's many priceless possessions is the oldest completely intact glass painting in the world, a small romanesque window dating back to 1140. The larger, Gothic stained windows (1330) and the imposing romanesque bronze door are also of great intrinsic value, as are the paintings for the Weingartner altar by Hans Holbein the Elder who, like his son Hans Holbein the Younger, was a native of Augsburg. The father lived in Augsburg for most of his life, but Holbein the Younger settled in London in 1530, becoming Henry viii's favourite artist, and died there at the age of 46 in 1543.

Hard by the High Cathedral and actually within its precincts are the former bishop's palace, disused since 1733, with its delightful garden, and the Fronhof, where jousts were held many centuries ago. Almost immediately opposite is the fifteenth-century home of Konrad Peutinger, the classical scholar and one-time keeper of the Augsburg archives, who lived there from 1465 until 1547. It was he who possessed the so-called *Tabula Peutingeriana*, said to be a fourth-century Roman military map and one of the oldest maps known. However, a number of experts have subsequently expressed the opinion that it is no more than a twelfth-century copy and that Peutinger must have been well aware of the fact. It was bought by Prince Eugene of Savoy in 1714 and now reposes in the National Library of Vienna. Facsimiles of it, reproduced in postcard form, may be bought from the Peutingerhaus and from a number of souvenir shops in the vicinity.

Returning down the Hoher Weg to the Augustus Fountain, you will find the Rathaus on your left. Built in 1620 by Elias Holl, it is the largest Town Hall in Central Europe and is claimed to be the most impressive example of the German

4   *Rothenburg ob der Tauber: view from the Röder Tower*

Renaissance style of architecture. Alongside it is the Perlach Tower (1618) from the top of which a magnificent view of Augsburg may be obtained. Behind the Rathaus and east of it are a number of buildings well worth seeing, including the Bar-füsser (Barefoot) Church, built in 1398 and one of the first Protestant churches in Bavaria, the St Maria-Stern Convent (1574), which has the first onion-shaped tower ever to be constructed, and the Jakobspfründe (Jacob's Prebend) founded in 1546.

The name Jakob (German for James) will be found associated with many buildings and institutions in Augsburg but, in many cases, it does not refer to the saint but to one Jakob Fugger, who lived here during the fifteenth and sixteenth centuries. He and his two brothers, Ulrich and Georg, became not only the town's wealthiest and most prominent citizens but also its greatest benefactors. The Fuggers were shrewd and far-sighted merchants, who recognised the value of Bavaria as a trade route between Germany and the south and built up an enormous business in handling goods to and fro. They ran what today would be the equivalent of a road haulage and import and export organisation and, in addition, they owned a fleet of merchant vessels plying between Trieste – to which the boundary of Bavaria then extended – and the Middle East. They traded largely in Oriental carpets, spices and fruits, as well as in gems and precious metals, and continued to prosper until the shipping route from Western Germany to the East via the Cape of Good Hope was opened up, after which the amount of commercial traffic passing through Bavaria gradually dwindled.

Their gifts and endowments to the people and town of Augsburg were manifold and one of their lasting benefices will be found today just past the Barfüsser Church, lying off to the right of the Jakoberstrasse. This is the Fuggerei, a completely self-contained village of quaint old houses, interspersed by quiet, tree-shaded streets and fountains, where more than 100 poor Catholics live in peace and contentment. Guidebooks and

5 *Rothenburg ob der Tauber: the Plönlein*

encyclopaedias usually describe the Fuggerei as 'the world's social settlement', but I heartily agree with Garry Hogg who, in his excellent book *Bavarian Journey*, says 'this is a bleak reference indeed'. The place is the work of one inspired by God and where else in the world could you rent a delightful little home for the same money that was paid in 1520? The annual tenancy is still one Rhenish Florin – today's equivalent being no more than one mark and 71 pfennigs or less than 20p!

For a number of years, the Fuggers were in danger of being outrivalled by the Welsers, although the latter family were by no means so dedicated to acts of charity. They were merchant bankers, alleged to be richer even than the Lombards and Medicis, and they devoted much of their great wealth to political manipulations, financing wars and interfering with elections. They also spent huge sums upon the exploration of South America and their representative, Federmann, literally *bought* most of Venezuela for the Welsers in 1528, despite the fact that it was occupied by the Spanish. The Welsers did not, however, remain leading lights in Augsburg for long. After a series of shattering financial crashes, they vanished into obscurity in 1614.

Another wide road, the Maximilianstrasse, stretches due south from the Rathaus and at its end you will find the Minster of St Ulrich, with its two onion towers. The towers are not identical – indeed, one is so much smaller than the other that you may not notice it at first – and they actually belong to two different churches joined together, one Protestant and the other Catholic. By this means, St Ulrich's exemplifies the Religious Peace of Augsburg which, in 1555, endeavoured to bring the two denominations together.

The Maximilianstrasse and the streets leading off it contain most of Augsburg's most interesting buildings. Leaving St Ulrich's and walking northwards, you will find an early eighteenth-century house on your left which was the home of Johannes Andreas Stein, one of the world's most famous organ builders. It was here that Mozart often stayed during his frequent visits to the town. The great composer was, of course, a native of Salzburg, but his father was born in Augsburg in a small house on the Frauentorstrasse, north of the Cathedral, and the people here have since come to look upon the son as a part of their inheritance. Mozart recitals are staged frequently in the town and the father's home is now a small museum containing many of the composer's prized possessions.

A short distance farther north, the Fountain of Hercules, designed by the Dutchman Adriaen de Vries in 1602, stands in the middle of the road. East of it lies the Weaver's Emporium, built by Elias Holl in 1611, with behind it the secularised Dominican Church. This is now a Roman Museum, containing many valuable relics, including a superb third-century gilded horses's head, which have been excavated in and around the city.

West of the Hercules Fountain is the Schaezlerpalais, a rococo festival hall built in 1770 by Lespilliez especially to receive Marie Antoinette on her way from Vienna to Paris to marry Louis XVI. How much wiser she would have been to have remained in peaceful Augsburg instead of ending her life on the guillotine 23 years later! Behind this building, in the Hallstrasse, is the massive former Dominican monastery, now an art gallery, with the old Customs House building – a busy place indeed in the times of the Fuggers – immediately opposite.

Continuing northwards, we arrive at the Fuggerhaus on our left. This was erected by Jakob Fugger in 1515 and was for many years afterwards the family seat. You should not fail to inspect the ladies' courtyard in this building, which has a curiously Italian appearance. The earlier Fuggers exhibited a strange attitude towards their womenfolk, keeping them cloistered from the outside world like nuns, and the courtyard was where they took most of their daily exercise.

A little farther up the Maximilianstrasse is the Fountain of Mercury, another example of de Vries's work and three years older than the Fountain of Hercules. It stands in front of the thirteenth-century Catholic church of St Moritz, which was Gothicised in 1535 and entirely rebuilt in 1950. It was once described to me as the ugliest ecclesiastical structure in Augsburg and I am inclined to agree with this opinion. However, you will find ample compensation for its lack of beauty if you take the turning immediately past it and walk westwards. Here you will find the beautiful sixteenth-century house of the patrician Koepf family, with its magnificent hall, and the one-time home of the Welsers, which is equally attractive. Beyond them is the lovely church of St Anne, founded as a Carmelite monastery in 1321, with its memorial chapel to the Fuggers.

The Fuggers were basically Catholics, so it is perhaps a little strange to discover their memorial in a strictly Protestant church. But it must be remembered that Jakob and his two brothers lived in the same day and age as Martin Luther, who came to Augsburg in the early part of the sixteenth century because he realised that many of the town's inhabitants, including the Fuggers, had Protestant sympathies. It was here that he settled down to preach his doctrine of the Reformed Religion, setting out his principles in the famous Confession of Augsburg of 1530. The great reformer found many ardent followers amongst the artists living in Augsburg at that time and one of them, Lukas Cranach, painted a fine portrait of Luther, which may also be seen in the church of St Anne.

Whilst on the subject of artists, I strongly recommend a visit to the house where Holbein the Elder lived and where the Younger was born. It will be found quite easily by taking the street passing in front of the St Maria-Stern Convent and continuing southwards for a short distance. Or, if you are in the Maximilianstrasse, you can take the turning to the north and east of the Hercules Fountain and carry straight through for about a quarter of a mile.

The house contains a number of works by both Holbeins but further examples will be found in the Dominican monastery behind the Schaezlerpalais. Here also are paintings by Burgmair, Apt, Breu, Zeitblom, Schaffner, Schäufelein and Strigel, all of whom had direct connections with Augsburg. And you will be fascinated by the magnificent portrait of Jakob Fugger by Albrecht Dürer, which is an exceptionally realistic work. Dürer, who was born in Augsburg in 1471, was the inventor of etching and is generally regarded as the founder of the German school.

One artist who was not of local origin but who spent several years in the town was the Italian master, Titian. He visited Augsburg at the invitation of Charles V and, whilst there, painted the portraits of many notabilities assembled for the peace conference, as well as the equestrian portrait of the Emperor now in the Prado Gallery, Madrid. He later became a favourite of Prince Philip of Spain and, when Philip succeeded to the throne, produced many of his classical 'poesies' for his royal patron.

Augsburg has several good theatres, the largest being the Stadttheatre in Kennedyplatz. But one that should on no account be missed is the Augsburger Puppenkiste by the Rotes Tor, where fascinating marionette shows are regularly staged. Nearby there is also an open-air theatre, with seating for 2,500 people, where operas and operettas are performed during June and July.

There are so many buildings and places of interest in Augsburg that it would take a whole volume to describe them all in full, and I have been able to mention only a comparative few of the outstanding ones. But if you have the time to spare, I strongly advise a tour of the old town walls and fortifications, which will be found intermittently along the whole length of the eastern boundary. Beginning at the Rotes Tor and passing the sixteenth-century Wool Market and church of St Margareth on your left, you proceed northwards along the Forsterstrasse until you come to the Vogeltor gate (1445) with its Gothic vaulting and St Ursula's church (1470). Now you strike off to the right along the Vogelmauer which will lead you to a covered sentry walk known as the Jakobwall (1540). A short distance to the north of this is the thirteenth-century Jakobtor, one of the earliest gates to be built. Continue along the Untere Jakobermauer and you will pass the Fünfgratturm (Five-Crested Tower) which was built in 1454 and arrive at Water Tower (1608) and Oblatterwall (1540). The road makes a sweeping detour around this and takes you into the Bert-Brecht-Strasse which opens out on to the Schwedenstiege (Swedish Staircase), with fortifications stretching to the right and left. This is a relic of the days when the Swedes occupied Bavaria for a short period. At the north end of the wall is the Catholic church of St Gallus, founded in 1051 and rebuilt in 1589. Cross the Stephingerberg here and a short walk will bring you to the Lueginsland bastion, which is at the northernmost point of the old town.

Perhaps I should not leave Augsburg without mentioning two of its more recent distinguished sons. Rudolf Diesel was born here in 1858 and much of the town's industry is still concerned with the engine he invented, although its practical value was not realised until 20 years after his death. And a name that must surely evoke many memories for years to come it that of Messerschmitt, a family who have lived in and around Augsburg for more than two centuries. Willy Messerschmitt, who was born in 1898, became interested in aircraft when in his early 20s and later became chief engineer of the Bayerische Flugwerke, afterwards founding the company which bears his name and which produced many thousands of military planes during the Second World War. The company was reconstituted in 1964 and, although Willy was not elected to its board of management, he was given the position of honorary chairman for life. The present Messerschmitt works are in Haunstetten, a suburb of Augsburg, employing some 5,000 people.

3. The Romantic Road Through Franconia

The so-called Romantic Road begins at Füssen in the Allgäu and runs through Augsburg to Würzburg, covering a distance of some 340 kilometres (212 miles). I say so-called deliberately because there has always been a certain element of doubt about the name. According to a number of old books I have read in various Bavarian town libraries, it was originally styled the Romanischeweg, or Roman Road, and I believe it must have acquired its present appellation through one of those printers' errors that frequently occurred in the textbooks of bygone days, the letter 't' creeping in by mistake and remaining there ever since. By a similar though reverse process, London's Convent Garden became transformed into Covent Garden, and there are countless other examples I could quote.

That the road was originally built and used by the Romans there can be no doubt. We know that the invaders came down through the Lechtal to Füssen and moved rapidly northwards to Augsburg, afterwards establishing a camp just south of Würzburg. And many of the Roman remains that have been discovered in Franconia came from places along the route. On the other hand, the Fuggers, with their impressive caravan-serais, their rich trading posts and their solicitude for the peoples who lived along their main commercial artery, most definitely added a touch of romance to what until their coming was a strongly fortified and frequently bellicose part of Bavaria,

So let us stick to Romantic Road; it has such a much nicer sound.

From Augsburg the road runs first to Donauwörth, but I suggest taking a detour through the old fortress town of Ingolstadt. It is well worth seeing, if only for its Liebfrauenkirche, which was built between 1425 and 1525 and which is claimed to be the largest basilica-type church in Bavaria. The town itself dates back to 806 and was the seat of the first state university. Its church of St Moritz, the ducal residence and the Herzogkasten, all that remains of the old castle, were built in the thirteenth century, whilst the amazingly well-preserved town walls, with more than 40 towers and gates, were constructed during the following 100 years. In the eighteenth-century church of Maria de Victoria, built by the Asam brothers, there is a magnificent ceiling painting.

Neuburg lies approximately halfway between Ingolstadt and Danauwörth and, like them, is on the Danube. The residence and castle were originally established in the eleventh century but were constructed in 1530-45 largely by Palgrave Ottheinrich. The castle chapel has frescoes by Hans Bocksberger (1543) and you will find some fine early sixteenth-century tapestries in the town's history museum.

It may perhaps come as something of a surprise to realise that all the towns in this area are some 1,400 feet above sea level. In fact, the whole of Bavaria is set high up, at altitudes ranging from 500 feet in the north to nearly 10,000 feet in the southern Alps. Incidentally and because of the mountains, the southernmost part of the country is known as Oberbayern (Upper Bavaria), a fact that many English visitors are inclined to find confusing at first.

Donauwörth makes a good apertif for the rich feast of medievalism that lies in store for all those who travel the Romantic Road. It stands not only on the Danube but also on the minor river Wörnitz which, in places, almost comes up to the town's walls. Its attractions include the fifteenth-century parish church with its sacrament house, the baroque Church of the Holy Cross, built in 1717-22 on the site of an old Benedictine monastery, and a remarkably curious gateway known as the Färbertörle, which could be literally translated as the 'little painted door'. Here also is yet another of the Fuggers' customs houses.

From Donauwörth it is only a short distance to Harburg, which is little more than a large village dominated by a massive and none too attractive twelfth–eighteenth-century castle, which looks rather like one of those revolting 'Grand Palace' hotels you find at some of the more popular English seaside resorts. But as a castle it has everything – covered parapets, keep, church, courtyards, knight's hall, dungeons, torture chambers, you name it – and it never fails to evoke squeals of delight from small children. Museum addicts will also find it well worth exploring, since it contains a magnificent collection of romanesque ivory carvings, some fine specimens of Gothic tapestry and statues by Tilman Riemenschneider. The library will also prove of special interest to bibliophiles; it has many well-preserved old manuscripts, besides rare incunabula of early copperplate prints.

I shall always remember Harburg as the place where, when I was very young, I met my first knight in shining armour. He was clanking his way unsteadily across the town's picturesque stone bridge and, although he was being pelted with stones by the local urchins, he was kind enough to stop and and present me with an extremely sticky toffee apple. A strange, strong odour wafted towards me through the vizor of his helmet and it was only years later that I realised he must have been blind drunk, having staggered all the way from Nördlingen after taking part in a pageant! Yet to me he will always remain the true, gentil and parfit knight.

More than 25 years later, I came across another strange apparition when driving from Harburg to Donauwörth one September evening. Out of the dusk in front of my headlights loomed an extraordinary figure that I thought at first could only be a ghost. On closer inspection, however, it revealed itself to be a human, clad in an incredibly grubby sheet and with a head completely enclosed in a large pumpkin in which slits had been cut for the eyes and mouth. I pulled up my car and the apparition approached my open side window, muttering excitedly.

Now the Franconian accent is difficult enough to understand at the best of times, but coming from within a pumpkin it was utterly incomprehensible. I had no idea what the fellow was saying, but I gathered from his gestures that he wanted a lift. I drove him into Donauwörth and, throughout the whole ten-minute journey, he kept up a running conversation to which I could only reply *Ja* and *Nein* at intervals and hope that I was on the right lines. The stench of the hollowed-out pumpkin persisted in my car for many days afterwards and I often wonder how he managed to breathe inside it without being sick.

Travelling north out of Harburg you soon arrive at Nördlingen, an unspoilt medieval town that happens to have the largest population of any place on the Romantic Road between Augsburg and Würzburg, although you would not think so. It is surrounded by a high wall – broken at intervals by no fewer than 15 gates and towers, with remarkable parapets that are accessible all along their length and covered by overhanging gabled roofs that provide very effective shelter from the weather. They run, rather like a high pavement, past the upper floors of the quaint little houses that line the inner side of the wall and, if you are not careful, you may find yourself peeping through a window and observing some intimate bedroom scene that was not meant for the eyes of a stranger!

Nördlingen has been described by some writers as 'the living medieval city' and I cannot fault this description. At dusk, when the narrow streets are rid of traffic, you could imagine yourself walking through London in Tudor times and, to add to the illusion, you will even hear two night watchmen calling to each other as the town clocks strike ten. Many of the peasants thronging the streets and market places during the day wear traditional costumes based on sixteenth-century designs and this also gives the impression that Nördlingen has turned back the pages of history.

St George's Church, constructed between 1427 and 1505, is typical of the late Gothic period and large enough to be mistaken for a cathedral. It is from its 300-foot tower – nicknamed Daniel by the inhabitants – that one of the watchmen cries at night. Inside the church is a fifteenth-century pulpit and a high altar dating from 1683.

You will notice, incidentally, that the name of St George crops up in association with many churches in Bavaria, particularly in the villages. Indeed, I am told that it arises more frequently in this context than it does in England. I doubt, however, whether it is the same St George whom Edward III adopted as the patron saint of England during the fourteenth century. A martyr by this name was known to and revered by the Bavarians from the time of their Christianisation and the first church dedicated to him was founded in Bavaria during the eleventh century. I rather fancy he must be the St George of the Eastern Christian Church – a Greek who was put to death by pagans *c*. A.D. 300.

As I shall be describing in a later chapter, the people of Traunstein in the Tirol organise a St George's Day Ride every year. And Nördlingen also stages a splendid annual pageant of a somewhat similar nature. This is the Scharlachrennen (Scarlet Race) – the oldest festival in Germany – when horse riders, clad in historical costumes, indulge in competition. There are also two other notable events – the Staben Festival, which takes place in May, and the Anno 1643 Pageant, commemorating the year when Nördlingen was under siege.

Thirty-two kilometres (20 miles) north of Nördlingen you will find yet another compact medieval town, Dinkelsbühl, which is considerably smaller and, in my opinion, much more beautiful. Unfortunately, the Romantic Road has been so highly publicised that, in high summer, most of its show places are overrun by seething mobs of tourists. But, somehow or other, Dinkelsbühl has managed to remain something of an oasis and you will find room to breathe here, even in mid-July.

Once again there is a St George's Church, founded a little later than the one in Nördlingen but similarly big enough to be a cathedral. It was designed and built by Nicolas Eseler, who must be rated amongst the immortals of Bavarian architecture, and its late Gothic beauty is breathtaking to behold. Another local architect of considerable repute was Matthew Binder, who built the nearby Deutschordenhaus in 1761-4 as a permanent headquarters for the Franconian knights of the Teutonic Order.

I feel I must digress at this point to say something about the Teutonic Order, since it was for a long while so closely associated with Bavaria. It was formed originally by the merchants of Bremen and Lübeck in the twelfth century to look after wounded Christians in the Crusades, in much the same way as the English founded the Order of St John of Jerusalem. In 1198, with full papal approval, it became a military order, the knights adopting the attire of a white mantle on which was described a black cross. Its troops suffered an overwhelming defeat at Tannenberg in 1410 and, in 1525, the Order was secularised in Prussia, after which its headquarters were moved to Franconia. It was heavily defeated again in the Thirty Years' War and, in 1809, all its properties were confiscated by the Austrians. It was reorganised in 1834 as a part religious, part military body and finally transformed into a mendicant order in 1929.

Not far from St George's Church is the celebrated Deutsches Haus, one of the most marvellous examples of half-timbered building I have ever seen. Dating from about 1600, it was first used as an inn, then became a centre of local trade and finally a seat of local government. It is surrounded on all sides by beautiful old-world buildings, which have been preserved in magnificent condition. Some of these are shops selling everyday modern goods and, on my last visit to Dinkelsbühl, I was greatly amused to discover an impressive display of television sets in the window of an establishment that bore the date 1536!

Every July, Dinkelsbühl stages a remarkable pageant called the Kinderzeche, which is a kind of thanksgiving for the town being saved from destruction during the Thirty Years' War. As its name implies, it is largely a festival for young people and, besides displays of traditional folk dancing, its programme includes concerts by the local boys' band, which is so good that it could easily compete on equal terms with some of the best adult municipal bands in the land.

A little farther along the road to Würzburg lies the small town of Feuchtwangen, even sleepier and quieter than Dinkelsbühl though nothing like as attractive. There is very little of historic interest to see here, but those people who are fond of studying local handicrafts will find a visit to the Heimatmuseum rewarding. And, of course, there is the usual wealth of old burgher houses. Open-air performances of plays are staged in the romanesque convent during the summer but, unless you have a good knowledge of German, you will find them exceedingly boring.

I would not include the next small town, Schillingfürst, except to recommend it as an ideal place in which to stay if you intend to linger in the area. Having nothing special to offer by way of local attractions, it is overlooked by the majority of tourists who travel the Romantic Road and, in consequence, its few small hotels and Gasthäuser do not charge exorbitant prices. The last time I stayed here, I was charged a pound a day for full pension in a delightfully clean and comfortable little inn and, at the time of writing, the price has remained unchanged. Schillingfürst has the advantages of being equidistant from both Würzburg and Nürnberg, each of these towns being approximately 90 kilometres (56 miles) away. It is also connected with them by rail.

When you arrive at Rothenburg ob der Tauber – which is 13

kilometres (eight miles) north of Schillingfürst – you will find yourself in what many people consider to be the most beautiful little town in the whole of Bavaria. It certainly has all the ingredients – walls, parapets, towers, fountains, steep gabled houses and cobbled side streets – but I fear much of its onetime attractiveness has been worn thin by what can only be described as blatant commercialism. In the summer months it is bedlam, with gaping trippers packing the narrow streets so tightly that it is almost impossible to walk through them, let alone drive. Many of the visitors come on organised day trips (I saw no fewer than 142 motorcoaches parked in Rothenburg on one July day recently!) and those who don't cram themselves into the comparatively few hotels and guesthouses – sometimes sleeping as many as five in one room – so that it is impossible to find accommodation unless you book well in advance. If you really want to enjoy Rothenburg in a reasonable amount of peace and quiet, you would be well advised to go there in the end of September or the beginning of May.

The town, like many others in Bavaria, was once an imperial free city. It is completely walled in and gives one the impression of having been built within the battlements of a huge castle. These fortifications were very necessary in the Middle Ages, because the citizens of Rothenburg were just as commercially minded then as they are today and their wealth was the envy of all those who invaded Franconia. Rothenburg was also for some time the seat of the mighty Hohenstauffens, an unruly family who spent their lives scrapping with all and sundry.

The oldest building standing today is probably the early twelfth-century chapel of St Blaize. It is quite small and was once attached to the ancestral castle of the Hohenstauffens, of which some remains are still to be seen. This castle has proved to be something of a mystery to historians, some of whom allege that it was raised on the site of what was once a Roman camp. There can be no doubt, however, that it was one of the first castles to be built in Western Bavaria if not actually *the* first. The interior of the chapel is extremely simple and contains remains of romanesque frescoes to which no precise date has yet been given.

The parish church of St James (Jakobskirche) was built in the years between 1371 and 1471. It contains a fine sacrificial altar, masterly carved by Tilman Riemenschneider in 1501-5, and a high altar dating back some 50 years earlier. The tabernacle (c. 1400) is one of its oldest interior features, although there is good reason to believe that the choir window might be earlier still. But oldest of all is undoubtedly a stone Madonna, which was sculpted in the mid-fourteenth century and transferred to the church from the Franciscan monastery nearby. The aisle was designed by Frederik Herlin.

The second most ancient building in Rothenburg is the Franciscan Church which formed part of the monastery to which I have just referred. It was founded between 1285 and 1309, though parts of it suggest that there may have been a small chapel on the site previously, and its churchyard contains the graves of the medieval Franconian nobility, some of whom have lain there for nearly 700 years.

The Rathaus is numbered amongst the five most famous town halls in all Germany. In effect, it could claim to be older than the Franciscan Church, since the Gothic portion of it goes back to 1240, but the gabled tower and the main Renaissance building were erected in the second half of the sixteenth century. They were largely the work of Leonard Weidmann, who was also responsible during the same period for the Hospital of the Holy Ghost, to be found in the courtyard of Hegereiter House close by. It is believed that Weidmann was to a great extent financed by the Fuggers and it is certain that they paid for much of the cost of the magnificent Baumeister House, which Weidmann completed in 1596 and which, like his work on the Town Hall, is in Renaissance style.

Rothenburg lies close to the upper stretch of the quiet river Tauber (Dove) and it is a little strange to realise that this peacefully named tributary of the Danube once flowed with blood during the Frankish invasion and, on another occasion, was held responsible for bringing the Black Death into Bavaria from Germany. If you wander for a short distance along the upper Tauber valley you will find the Topplerschlösschen, a medieval defence tower now filled with curious antique furniture, and the village of Detwang, which has a church containing a remarkable cruciform altar by Tilman Riemenschneider.

Every year at Whitsuntide, Rothenburg stages an elaborate performance called *Der Meistertrunk* (literally translated 'The Master Drink') which is as good enough excuse as any for the inhabitants to get drunk. It dates back to 1631, when the town was besieged and the enemy commander ordered it to be totally destroyed. He then agreed to spare it on the condition that one of the burghers should down three litres of wine (nearly three-quarters of a gallon!) at a single draught. The town's mayor, an old man of seventy named Nusch, accepted the challenge and achieved the tremendous feat with comparative ease. His masterly accomplishment is also perpetuated by *Der Meistertrunk* clock, which you will find near the Rathaus and which plays daily at 11, 12, 1 and 2.

On the main road north and not far from Detwang lies Creglingen. It is a very unimpressive village and most motorists drive straight through it without giving it a single thought. Yet in its modest Herrgotts Church is one of the greatest masterpieces ever created by Tilman Riemenschneider – his intricate high altar depicting the Ascension of the Holy Virgin. Carved during the first half of the sixteenth century, it is unpainted and seven metres (nearly 23 feet) high. You will be missing a truly memorable experience if you do not visit it.

Finally, on the last leg of our journey along the Romantic Road, we come to Bad Mergentheim, the 'town with two lives'. For nearly three hundred years, from 1525 to 1809, the Teutonic knights lived here and it was their main headquarters until more than half of the Order moved to Dinkelsbühl at the end of the

6   *Würzburg: the east façade of the Residenz*

eighteenth century. Their castle residence still stands on the south bank of the Tauber, although it was not in a very good state of repair the last time I visited it.

After Napoleon dissolved the Order and its properties were confiscated by the Austrians, Mergentheim literally died, many of its inhabitants and particularly its tradespeople moving farther afield. And then, in 1827, a shepherd named Franz Gehrig found mineral springs close to the north bank of the river. There were four springs in all, each of them proving to have distinct healing properties.

These were the days when the wealthy people of Europe, oversated with food and drink, were seeking 'the cure' here, there and everywhere; when every town and village that could claim a water of special quality was opening up as a *spa* or a *bad*. Almost overnight a new Mergentheim rose around the springs that had been so providentially discovered and, by the middle of the century, *Bad* Mergentheim had become accepted as a health resort. Archaeologists have since discovered that the springs were active in the late Iron Age and there is some evidence to show that their properties were known to the Romans.

And so to Würzburg, the fifth largest city in Bavaria and the second in industrial importance. It will always remain to me a sad reminder of the utter futility of indiscriminate warfare. I visited it first in 1937 and, when I returned ten years later, I was almost driven to tears by the scene of utter devastation that met my eyes. Much has been said and written about the bombing of Coventry on 14 November 1940, but it pales into insignificance compared with what happened in Würzburg on the night of 16-17 March 1945. The whole city fell victim to one of the largest concentrations of Allied bombers ever mobilised and, in less than six hours, four-fifths of it was completely destroyed by fire. But the irony of the whole tragic episode was that the target set for the raiders, the several large engineering works on the outskirts of the town, suffered the least damage of

7   *Würzburg: the Kaiser Saal in the Residenz*

all. I know this to be true, because I saw it with my own eyes. Perhaps we shall never know who was directly responsible for this futile operation but, on 9 March 1947, I would have liked to have rubbed his nose in the dust of a cathedral that was far older and more beautiful than the one in Coventry.

Today, thanks to the industry and devotion of the people of Würzburg, the town looks very much as it did before the war, except that one detects new paintwork and new masonry almost everywhere one looks. However, they resisted the temptation to erect a structure of modern design on the site of the cathedral and have restored it beautifully to its original form, using as much of the ancient bricks and woodwork as could be salvaged. This is also true of most of the city's other historic buildings that were razed to the ground.

The Cathedral Church of St Kilian – to give it its proper name – was founded in 1188, but it was not raised, as some guidebooks state, over the grave of the Irish missionary Kilian who, with his compatriots Kolonat and Totnan, first brought Christianity to the area. His tomb will be found in the crypt of the Neumünster, which stands almost adjacent to the cathedral. Kolonat and Totnan are also buried here.

One of the features of the cathedral that remained virtually intact after the bombing is the Schönborn funeral chapel. This some fine sculptures by Claude Curé. Otherwise, you will find some fine sculptures by Claude Cure. Otherwise, you will find more features of interest in the Neumünster, which suffered less damage and still retains many of its original treasures, including some fine carvings by Riemenschneider. The Neumünster, originally romanesque and converted to baroque in 1710-20 by Joseph Greising, was formerly an abbey and many church dignitaries lie buried in its cloister courtyard, now known as the Lusamgärtlein. Here also lies the famous Minnesinger, Walther von der Vogelweide, who became a monk in his latter years.

Wherever you go in Würzburg you will find statues of the Madonna. There were nearly 500 of them before the war and, when the city was rebuilt, those remaining were given places of honour on the house fronts, in addition to some that have been carved or sculpted during the 1950s. I believe there are now about 300 in all.

This obsession with the Madonna dates back to medieval times, when the devout people of Würzburg placed their town in the care of the Holy Mother. It is reflected in the statue of the 'Patrona Franconiae', which stands on the fifteenth-century bridge spanning the river Main, and in the names of the town's parish church – the Marienkapelle – and the fortress of Marienberg, which was once the residence of the prince-bishops. Within this fortress, too, is the Chapel of the Virgin Mary, built in 706 and the oldest church east of the Rhine.

The history of Würzburg has never been clearly defined. At one time it was said to have begun with the Celts, but recent excavations in and around the town seem to indicate that there were people living here more than 100,000 years ago. Certainly the Celts came to occupy the area later in great numbers, many of them living in the vicinity of the hill on which the Marienberg fortress stands. It has not been definitely established whether the Romans ever camped in Würzburg, though some Roman remains have been found not far to the south. What is certain, however, is that Würzburg was one of the first towns in Bavaria to be Christianised and, in 1741, after the spadework put in by Kilian, Kolonat and Totnan, its first bishopric was founded by St Boniface, who had been archbishop and primate of Germany since 732. Boniface was, in fact, an Englishman, having been born either in or near about Crediton, in Devon, c. 675. He resigned his archbishopric in 753 and resumed work as a missionary, finally being murdered by heathens in Dokkum, in the Netherlands. A sorry end for one who had done so much to teach the Christian faith to the people of Germany.

Würzburg has produced many great ecclesiastics during the past 1,200 years, but it has also fostered some outstanding artist-craftsmen, including Tilman Riemenschneider. We have already encountered examples of his work during our journey along the Romantic Road and I think the time has now come to mention something about him. Born in Osterode, Saxony, in 1460, he came to Würzburg at the age of 23 and set up business as a 'journeyman painter'. This particular designation covered a multitude of activities, ranging from straightforward house-painting to the execution of busts and portraits. Riemenschneider became much respected by the people of Würzburg, who elected him first a councillor and then their mayor. But he committed a grievous error in 1525 by siding with the peasants in their rebellion against the prince-bishops and was imprisoned in the fortress of Marienberg. By that time the churches of Franconia and Swabia were filled with his carvings, although neither Regensburg nor Nürnberg were prepared to tolerate what their contemporary art experts described as his 'childish execution'. His growing fame soon won him a pardon from the prince-bishop and he was released from prison in 1526 to die five years later. His carvings, almost entirely in linden wood and devoid of any gilding or colouring, are now held to be some of the finest of their kind in Europe if not in the world, and Tilman Riemenschneider is today accepted as one of the leading exponents of the German Gothic school.

Würzburg also produced the great Balthasar Neumann, who was largely responsible for rebuilding or restoring many of the town's oldest buildings during the eighteenth century and for converting them to the baroque style. Considered to be one of the foremost architects of his day and age, Neumann was originally a military engineer in the service of the prince-bishop, entrusted with the repair and maintenance of all the fortifications and churches within the see. He showed considerable creative aptitude at an early age and, when still in his 30s, became Professor of Architecture at Würzburg University. He died at the age of 70 in 1753.

Almost immediately opposite the main entrance of Würzburg Cathedral is the Domstrasse, which leads straight down to the old bridge over the Main, passing on its way the Grafeneckart, which has been the Town Hall since 1316. Mercifully spared from serious bomb damage, the bridge is 200 metres (650 feet) long and was rebuilt on the site of a previous structure in 1473. It is a wonderful example of medieval craftsmanship, with its buttressed piers and statues of saints on both sides. The river Main, incidentally, is the largest tributary of the Rhine, which it joins at Mainz, some 200 kilometres (125 miles) in a direct line from Würzburg. It is 490 kilometres (307 miles) long and navigable for a little over two-thirds of this length by barges up to 1,200 tons.

Turning left after crossing the bridge will bring you to the romanesque church of St Burchard – appointed Würzburg's first bishop by St Boniface and, like him, an Englishman by birth – beyond which the fortress of Marienberg stands austere and aloof on its small hill. The earliest part of this building, which was used as a residence by St Burchard, belongs to the eighth century. Since then, it has undergone many alterations and additions, the latest of which were by Neumann. I say the latest with a certain degree of caution, because Marienberg was almost completely gutted by fire during the 1944 attack and Neumann's work has since been restored by more modern hands. Nearly all of its priceless interior furnishings were burnt beyond recall.

Besides the circular Chapel of the Virgin Mary, to which I have already referred, the fortress now contains the Mainfränkisches Museum, which houses an outstanding collection of pictures, sculptures and tapestries from the Main and Franconian areas. When I last saw it, it was something of a glorious jumble, but I was assured that it would be 'regularised' in the course of time. I am told that the curator has described the museum as being 'a home for all Franconia's homeless works of art' and I can well believe it.

The fortress possesses a very deep well that is said to have sinister connections and also a tower called the Sonnenturm, where the old treasury and archives used to be kept and in which Riemenschneider was imprisoned.

Marienberg remained the seat of the prince-bishops with their retinues from the thirteenth century to the middle of the eighteenth, when they removed themselves to the infinitely more convenient and opulent surroundings of the magnificent new Residenz, built for them between 1720 and 1744 by Balthasar Neumann, Maximilian von Welsch and Lukas von Hildebrandt. The money for this extravagance was raised by the simple process of imposing a tax upon the citizens over a period of 25 years. If they refused or failed to pay it, they were automatically committed to prison!

You will find the Residenz by walking down the Hofstrasse, east of the cathedral, which takes you straight into the Residenzplatz. The building was also badly damaged by fire, but its imposing marble staircase with a ceiling fresco by Giovanni Battista Tiepolo miraculously survived, as did the same artist's painted ceiling in the residence's Emperor's Hall. This is such a wild and wonderful mixture of noblemen, saints, cherubs, angels, nude females and soldiers in armour that it usually reduces the more flippant observer to a state bordering upon hysteria. But, like the rather more restrained John Zink frescoes in the Count's Hall, it is none the less a fine work of art.

During the summer, Mozart concerts are held in the Emperor's Hall, lit by thousands of candles, and also in the gardens of the Residenz. And, in one wing of the building, you will find the *Weinpalais*. Würzburg has acquired considerable renown with its fine ales and vintage wines and every year there is a Vintners' Festival during the end of September and beginning of October. The quaint baroque *Kapelle*, another of Neumann's creations, is recognised as the vintners' church and has given its name to a fine wine. It stands amidst woods across the Main and to the south of Marienberg and contains many curious pavilion chapels with ceiling frescoes by Matthew Günther. If you are someone who really enjoys a good full-bodied wine that is not too dry, let me recommend Würzburg's *Stein, Leisten* or *Teufelskeller.*

If you continue down the Ottostrasse, south of the Residenzplatz, you will come to the new university building at the corner of the Sanderring. It is now one of Europe's leading universities, attended by some 10,000 students from all parts of the world. Würzburg has been a notable seat of learning ever since the early sixteenth century, gaining particular fame for the teaching of arts and sciences. One of the earliest medical schools was founded, together with the old university, by the prince-bishop Julius Echter between 1576 and 1592 and the old buildings, despite suffering severe bomb damage, still stand off the Juliuspromenade, a few hundred yards to the north of the Neumünster. Döllinger, the theologian who tried to reform the Catholic Church, was a graduate of Würzburg, as was the Great German philosopher Schelling (1775-1854), whilst Rudolf Virchow was its Professor of Pathological Anatomy in the mid-nineteenth century. And it was here that Wilhelm Konrad Röntgen discovered the x-ray in 1895.

There remain two other buildings that should on no account be missed by the visitor. In the truly delightful market place, a short distance to the north-east of the Neumünster, you will find the Marienkapelle, a very imposing Gothic building with its ornate spire and three towering naves, although the shops clustered around its base seem a trifle out of place. It was originally built in 1377 and contains some interesting tombs, including that of Balthasar Neumann, who himself proposed the designs for his own memorial only a few months before his death.

Immediately next door to the Marienkapelle and separated from it by a narrow passageway is the *Haus zum Falken*, a splendid example of rococo work. It was for many centuries an inn and meeting place for visiting merchants and, in 1751, it was entirely rebuilt as a luxurious hostelry, being what could be regarded as a prototype for today's multi-star hotels. It now houses the city's extremely comprehensive Public Library, also the Tourist Information Office where, as usual, you can obtain plenty of helpful advice and free literature about the town and its environs.

4. Bamberg and Bayreuth: A Study in Contrasts

The river Main makes a curious detour in Franconia, plunging southwards at Schweinfurt for a distance of about 40 kilometres and then, at Ochsenfurt, rising sharply north for another 50 kilometres. It thus forms an U-shaped loop, with Würzburg lying on its left arm, not far from the bottom. It is on this stretch of the river, together with the stretch between Schweinfurt and Bamberg, that most of Bavaria's best vineyards are to be found and, in consequence, the Franconians have dubbed it the *Bocksbeutelstrasse* (Bocksbeutel Road), naming it after their most popular wine.

My father, who was a sporting parson with a keen palate for vintages, preferred to call it the Rheumatic Road. He always maintained that the Franconian wines were but a feeble imitation of their Rhenish counterparts and that they caused large quantities of uric acid to build up in the body which was why nature had kindly provided Bavaria with a surfeit of mineral springs and why the Bavarians were always rushing off to take 'the cure'. There may be some truth in this, though I have never personally suffered any adverse after-effects from drinking Franconian wine. But perhaps I haven't consumed it in sufficient quantities. However, I have noticed that hardened Bavarian drinkers tend to supplement their wine with mineral water, so maybe they are being wise *before* the event.

Most of the wines emanating from the Upper Main are of

the white variety and, in any case, I would not recommend the red except for cooking purposes. *Bocksbeutel* is probably the safest choice, being neither too sweet nor too dry, and *Teufelskeller* is definitely one of the aristocrats. However, if you consider yourself to be something of a connoisseur, you should go a short distance down river from Würzburg to the village of Escherndorf and taste what they have to offer there. Despite my father's somewhat deprecating remarks about Franconian wines in general, I consider *Eschendorfer* to be one of the finest in Europe.

Schweinfurt, with a population that is growing almost as large as that of Würzburg, is the only other large town on the Bocksbeutel Road and as good a place as any in which to sample the Franconian wines. It is mainly devoted to heavy industries and specialises in the manufacture of ball bearings, which were actually invented here towards the end of the nineteenth century. It also carries on with its age-old business of dyeing and the production of dye-stuffs and has given its name to a shade of green used by colourists all over the world. Its factories were heavily bombed during the war, but the old buildings in the centre of the town escaped damage and its market place is especially worthy of mention. It contains a fine statue of Friedrich Ruckert, the famous German poet who was born here in 1788.

There is an excellent train service from Schweinfurt to Bamberg (the journey by express takes little more than half an hour) but, if you are fortunate enough to be motoring, you will find the road following the Main absolutely fascinating. It is dotted with picturesque little villages – each of which has its own local wine to offer – and most of them have quaint old inns in which you can obtain a good but simple meal for a very modest price. If you have not already been struck by Bavaria's curious inn-signs, you cannot fail to notice them all along this route. They are mostly beautifully wrought in iron, consisting of a wreath surrounding a gilded emblem denoting the name of the house – a bull, a dove, a stag's head and so forth. Many of the inns have painted fronts depicting stages in the making of wine.

It was in one of these villages that I was once forcibly reminded of the proverb 'a good wine needs no bush'. The time was early October and the local innkeeper had suspended a vine bush from his sign to indicate that he was now able to supply the current vintage. I went inside and was served with a glass of cloudy yellow liquid that looked not unlike Devonshire scrumpy. It was a virgin wine straight from the press – what the French call *mût* and we call *must* – and, although it tasted all right, it subsequently reacted upon me like a strong dose of castor oil!

About half way between Schweinfurt and Bamberg you will come to Hassfurt, a small medieval town with ancient gate towers and an air of having gone to sleep and not wanting to be disturbed. You will find it worth while taking a look at the fifteenth-century Gothic Knight's Chapel and inspecting its collection of Franconian coats of arms. There are more than 200 of them altogether.

The district around Hassfurt abounds in castles of all shapes and sizes, and you will see quite a few of them as you travel along the road. I cannot tell you how many castles there are in Bavaria altogether – though I have been informed that they number between 2,000 and 3,000 – but I can assure you that, in all my travels through Europe, I have never come across any other country with such a profusion. And, on the road between Bamberg and Coburg, over a distance of not much more than 30 kilometres, I myself have counted more than 50. They demonstrate very vividly how much the medieval Bavarian landowners feared invasion and how determined they were to protect their families and their property.

A great many of these castles are still kept in excellent condition. Quite a number of them are now used as museums and some, still privately owned, have been converted into hotels.

They do not generally offer such sumptuous comfort and amenities as you will find elsewhere, but they are scrupulously clean and have the advantage of being very inexpensive. Any information office in Bavaria will be glad to give you further details about them, as will the excellent German Tourist Office in London.

Just outside of Bamberg, the river Regnitz joins the Main and here also begins the important canal that links the Rhine with the Danube by way of the Main and the Regnitz. It is of fairly recent construction, having been started in 1922 on the site of the older and much less effective Ludwig Canal, which had been slowly deteriorating since the end of the nineteenth century. During the war, Hitler soon realised the importance of the canal as a means of transporting arms and supplies to the eastern front and, in consequence, it received considerable attention from the Allied bombers. It is now in full operation again, travelling south down the Regnitz valley, by-passing Nürnberg at Furth and joining the Danube west of Regensburg after having traversed a distance of about 150 kilometres. By its means, barges of well over 1,000 tons can now pass from the North Sea to the Black Sea.

Canal boating holidays have recently been growing in popularity, especially on the Continent, and I have frequently been asked whether it is possible to explore Bavaria by this means. The answer is yes – always provided that you have sufficient time. To journey by river and canal from Würzburg in the north-west to Passau in the south-east will take you the best part of a week, so long as you cover at least 40 kilometres a day, and there is always the journey back to be taken into account. But, if you are prepared to devote a whole month to this exercise, you will be able to linger and to visit some of the loveliest places in the country. Small barges, equipped with washing and cooking facilities and able to accommodate from six to 10 passengers, may be hired in both Würzburg and Regensburg at rates that start from £4 a day or £80 a month and the owners will usually expect a deposit to cover the hire and insurance. The barges are powered by small diesel engines and you should allow 30 litres of fuel for every 100 kilometres covered. Here again, the German Tourist Office in London will provide you with all the necessary information.

Both the canal and the river Regnitz flow through Bamberg, but the town's most ancient buildings are concentrated around the latter, at a point where it splits and then rejoins, forming a small island on which stands the former Geyerswörth Castle (1585), which used to be the summer residence of the prince-bishops of Bamberg. A bridge, the Nonnenbrücke, leads off the island to the Schillerplatz, where stands the one-time home of the writer E. T. W. Hoffmann and the memorial Hoffmann Theatre. Hoffmann, besides being responsible for many books, was once the musical director of Bamberg's city theatre and was immortalised by Offenbach in his *Tales of Hoffmann*.

Immediately upstream, at the actual point where the river splits, is the Obere Brücke (Upper Bridge) athwart of which lies the magnificent Rathaus, a fifteenth-century building reconstructed in 1749-54 with foundations resting on another, much smaller island. Its curious position, midway between the banks of the Regnitz, arises from the fact that it had to deal with the administration of both halves of the old city. It can certainly be described as the most remarkable town hall in the whole of Germany and it is a splendid example of contemporary Bavarian architecture. Note, as you cross the bridge, the fascinating crucifixion scene on one of its parapets, the work of the sculptor Gollwitzer in 1715.

Directly above the Rathaus is another bridge, from which you can get a fine view of the cluster of fishermen's cottages on the east bank of the river. They have been aptly named Bamberg's 'Little Venice' and have become a sitting target for every tourist possessed of a camera. So much so that I actually found a coloured picture postcard of them in Tokyo not many years ago!

West of this bridge is what was once known as the Bishop's

City, the oldest and most historic quarter of Bamberg. Like Würzburg and Schweinfurt, Bamberg was also badly bombed, but this area was providentially spared. In the Dominikanstrasse, leading towards the cathedral, you will find the former Dominican Church, now the home of the Bamberg Symphony Orchestra. Its monastery and cloisters were built in the fourteenth century. Turning left shortly after leaving it will bring you into the Karolinenstrasse and face to face with the Emperor Cathedral with its four rather austere spires, each surmounting a fine romanesque portal, beautifully decorated with carved figures and reached by a wide flight of stone steps. The Domplatz in which the cathedral stands is breathtaking in its architectural superbity and has been described – I think very rightly – as 'the finest square in all Germany'.

The cathedral was founded in 1004 by the Holy Roman Emperor Henry II, King of Germany, and was consecrated on his birthday in 1012. It was twice destroyed by fire during the twelfth and thirteenth centuries and was finally rebuilt in its present form in 1237. Unlike many other ecclesiastical buildings in Bavaria, it did not undergo any marked changes during the Renaissance period.

In the Gothic west chapel is a real curiosity – the only papal tomb in Germany, that of Pope Clement II, who was originally Bishop Suidger of Bamberg and chancellor to the Holy Roman Emperor. He was called to the Holy See in 1046, died a year later and finally laid to rest in Bamberg after his remains were exhumed in 1235. Some years ago, doubts were raised as to his burial here and his tomb was opened. His partially embalmed body was found still clad in its papal robes, which were removed to the Diocesan Museum nearby. They are in a remarkably well preserved condition considering they are getting on for 1,000 years old.

The centre aisle contains the tomb of the Emperor Henry II and his consort Cunigunde, both of whom were buried here in the eleventh century, although the monument itself was not erected until 1513, being another of the works of Tilman Riemenschneider. It bears reliefs depicting scenes from the lives of Henry and his queen, but they are rather poorly executed and certainly not shining examples of the artist's craftsmanship. There is a story to the effect that Riemenschneider was forced to accept a low fee from the prince-bishop commissioning the work and, as a result, entrusted much of it to one of his pupils.

On the other hand, there are some truly magnificent medieval sculptures in the north side aisle which have gained worldwide recognition, including the Bamberger Rider, Mary and Elizabeth, Synagogue and Ecclesia. The names of those responsible for these works have never been ascertained, but they undoubtedly deserve a place in the gallery of fame. Further items to be admired are the choir screen with its superb relief work, the Maria or Christmas altar by Veit Stoss (1523) and the tomb of Bishop Friedrich of Hohenlohe which dates back to the mid-fourteenth century.

Next door to the cathedral is the Chapter House, rebuilt by Balthasar Neumann in 1730 and now the Diocesan Museum. This contains not only the robes of Pope Clement II but also those of Emperor Henry II and his Empress. In addition, there are a number of fine sculptures and other ecclesiastical relics which used to stand in the cathedral itself. It would appear that there was a great clearing out of statues, pictures and even altars some years back when it was considered by those in authority that the cathedral was, firstly, getting too cluttered up to be comfortable and, secondly, tempting would be thieves with too many easily portable articles of value!

From the Chapter House, you go down a short, narrow passage to the Old Imperial Court, a former royal and episcopal residence, part of which was once a fortress dating from the eleventh century. The inner courtyard is quietly grandiose, surrounded by half-timbered, balconied buildings with huge tiled roofs out of which three tiers of dormer windows peep at intervals. Inside you will find the remains of the old Diet Hall, where the local parliament sat for more than 500 years after 1085. The gabled Ratsstube, now the History Museum, is hard by, so is the Reiche Tor (Imperial Gate) with its delightfully sculpted figures surmounted by the Imperial coat of arms. The Ratsstube was where parliament assembled after the Diet Hall fell into disuse at the end of the sixteenth century.

In 1703 the prince-bishop and his entourage left the outmoded quarters of the Imperial Court and moved across the Domplatz to the massive, baroque New Residence, which had been made ready for use on 1 May. The prince-bishop – the fabulously wealthy Franz von Schönborn, who was also Archbishop and Elector of Mainz and one of the largest landowners in Bavaria – had not only paid for the building out of his own pocket but had also been largely responsible for its design, entrusting the final carrying out of the project to the architect Leonhard Dientzenhofer. Thereafter it became the official residence of all succeeding prince-bishops, who were also able to enjoy the sanctuary of its beautiful rose garden.

The New Residence, which today seems to be the main pride and joy of Bamberg's citizens, now houses the State Gallery. It contains some truly remarkable pictures, not all of which are to most people's tastes, including a terrifying representation of the Flood by Hans Baldung Grien. The ark is shown as a boxlike structure, heavily barred and not unlike an old-fashioned safe in appearance, which certainly couldn't have housed Noah and his family comfortably, let alone a collection of all the earth's fauna, male and female. It is surrounded by men, women and children, all in various stages of nudity and despair and all wallowing in turbulent flood waters together with their household chattels, whilst a young man in surprisingly modern-looking bathing trunks tries to force an entry, presumably for himself alone. The picture is certainly worth seeing, if only for its utter monstrosity!

8   *Würzburg: putti in the garden of the Residenz*

From the rose garden you will get a view of Bamberg's high-est point, away to the north-west, on which stands the imposing St Michael's Church, formerly a Benedictine Abbey founded by Henry II in 1015. To reach it you must head westwards down the Oberkarolinenstrasse then, when you come to the square facing the baroque St Jakob's Church, turn right into the Michaelsbergstrasse and walk first downhill and then uphill. You will then be confronted by the Abbey cloisters with St Michael's standing behind them. It was first built during the eleventh and twelfth centuries and the baroque façade above the balustraded stairway leading to the main entrance was added by Leonhard Dientzenhofer in 1697.

Inside the church are many treasures, including a magnificent pulpit by George Adam Reuss (1751) and a fantastic ceiling on which are depicted no fewer than 600 different medicinal herbs, most of them so rare that only a real expert can put a name to them. St Otto, the Pomeranian emissary to Bamberg who died here in 1139, has his tomb in the church as do many Bamberg bishops whose remains were removed from the cathedral from time to time and during the 'cleaning-up operation. The remain-ing monastery buildings, largely rebuilt by Balthasar Neumann and the Dientzenhofer brothers, later became almshouses and are now used as an old people's home.

There are many other historic buildings well worthy of a visit, but two you must make a point of seeing are the Böttinger House and the Concordia. These were respectively the winter and summer residences of the opulent and eccentric Franconian chargé d'affaires, Böttinger, who at one time considered himself to be the supreme ruler of Bamberg and who spent many years waging a private war against Prince-Bishop von Schönborn.

You will come across this custom of double residences where-ever you go in Bavaria and you will doubtless be surprised by the fact that the summer residence is often only a short distance away from the winter one. The reason may be found in Bavaria's climate which, since the country lies for the most part on a

9 *Würzburg: the bridge over the Main and the fortress of Marienberg*

high plateau, can be incredibly warm from mid-May to mid-September and freezingly cold from mid-November to mid-March. So the winter home was built of much sterner stuff than the summer home and liberally endowed with open fires and other heating appliances. There was also a subsidiary but equally practical second reason. The houses of the Bavarian nobility were so large and so crowded with diplomatic staff, personal body-guards and servants that they were extremely difficult to keep clean and to maintain. Thus their occupants moved from one residence to the other every six months in order that the vacated premises could be turned inside out, repainted and repaired. Finally, it was desirable to site both houses in the same town so that their owner could go about his daily business without having to commute from outside.

The Böttinger House, said to be the work of Leonhard Dientzenhofer but possibly attributable to his brother Georg, was completed in 1713 and is often claimed to be the finest baroque residence in all Bavaria, though I personally don't find it as superb as Bamberg's New Residence. It lies at the foot of the Judenstrasse, just south-east of the cathedral and on a site where the old ghetto once stood. The Jews, perpetually a butt of the German aristocracy, were banished from Bamberg during the sixteenth and seventeenth centuries and their ghetto was burnt to the ground.

A little further on, at the extreme end of the Concordiastrasse, you will find the Concordia itself, a baroque palace with parts of its base washed by the waters of the Regnitz, built in 1716-22 by Johann Dientzenhofer, the youngest of the three architect brothers. There is a certain amount of mystery surrounding its name. Some historians believe that it celebrates the Peace of Utrecht, but I personally think that the 'concord' celebrates the termination of the vendetta between Böttinger and the prince-bishop!

The history of Bamberg goes farther back than that of most other Bavarian towns, although it cannot claim to be older than

Würzburg. There is evidence of settlements having been here in the Stone Age and in the second century B.C. An old document reveals that it was called Castrum Babenberg in A.D. 902 and that most of its inhabitants had become Christians by that time. The cathedral school was already well established as a centre of learning before the beginning of the twelfth century. It was not until November 1802 that the Prince-Bishopric was finally secularised and added to Bavaria, but Bamberg remained almost untouched by this change of status. Since the beginning of the twentieth century a number of important industries have sprung up in the environs, one of the most notable being the Bosch auto-electrics organisation.

I feel that no loyal Englishman, having once arrived in Bamberg, could resist the temptation to travel a short distance north and visit the town of Coburg, now almost on the border of that gloomiest of all gloomy Communist countries, the German Democratic Republic. Because it was Coburg – sometimes called 'the cradle of European monarchy' – that produced the great great grandfather of Queen Elizabeth II, Albert of Saxe-Coburg-Gotha. The memorials that have been erected to the memory of Victoria's beloved Consort in England are all in incredibly bad taste and the statue of him that stands in Coburg's market square is no exception. I have forgotten who designed it, but it really doesn't matter.

The huge fortress (Veste Coburg) stands high above the town and is alleged to be one of the largest castles in Germany, if not in the world. Many members of the Saxe-Coburg antecedents were born within its walls during the Middle Ages, but later the family moved to the much smaller and more pleasant Schloss Rosenau, just outside the town, and it was here that Prince Albert first saw the light of day in 1819. As he grew up, he also spent some time in the Schloss Ehrenburg in Coburg, which was the family's winter residence.

The Veste – like so many buildings of its kind – now houses a museum. It contains some valuable pictures, including some little-known works by Dürer and Rembrandt, and some fine examples of period furniture. On the steep road leading up to the Veste you will find Coburg's Natural History Museum, which houses the biggest collection of stuffed birds I have ever seen in my life. My father, who detested all forms of taxidermy, once described it as 'a boarding-house nightmare'!

Another, much more interesting museum is to be found in Neustadt, a small town just to the north-east of Coburg and almost literally within spitting distance of the border. Here children's dolls have been manufactured for nearly five centuries and the museum contains more than 1,000 different specimens culled through the ages, all attired in contemporary folk costumes.

If you happen to be in Neustadt at noon, don't be surprised if you hear a goat bleating from somewhere above your head. This is the Rathaus clock, which happens to *strike* midday in this manner. There is a very long and involved story attached to this, which I do not intend to discuss in any great detail, but it seems that the 'baas' – now electronically produced – are in memory of a certain Neustadt tailor who, when the town was besieged in the Middle Ages, saved it from destruction by dressing himself up as a goat, thus convincing the enemy that the people still had plenty of food. All I can say is that military intelligence in those days must have been even worse than it is now!

Should you wish to stay and explore this region – and you will find it well worth your while – let me recommend Kronach, about 25 kilometres east of Coburg, as your headquarters. It is a very quaint, peaceful little town where they charge you very reasonably for board and lodging, and its inhabitants are most friendly and obliging. It has also the distinction of possessing one of the very few castles in Bavaria that were never captured by invaders and of being within a quarter of an hour's bus drive of Kulmbach, where they produce the finest beer in the country.

It is also the centre for some of the loveliest forest walks that may be found anywhere.

If you decide to take a trip from Kronach to Kulmbach to sample the ale, try and do so at the end of July when they stage their annual Beer Week. But please travel by bus and lock your car away if you have one. Some of the brews with which you will be eagerly plied have the kick of a mule!

There is another very large castle in Kulmbach, the Schloss Plassenburg. This was the seat of the margraves from 1397 until 1602 and was lavishly reconstructed by Caspar Vischer and Daniel Engelhardt in 1559-85. Lovers of tin soldiers will find within its walls some 10,000 metal figures representing not only members of the military but mankind in all his stages of evolution. Close to the castle is the sixteenth-century Schönerhof, which possesses one of the finest Renaissance jousting courts, and the Luitpold Museum with a collection of gold plate that was hidden during the Thirty Years' War and not rediscovered until 1912, nearly three centuries later.

A fat little Bavarian doctor once assured me that had it not been for Wagner there would have been no Bayreuth. To which I felt compelled to reply, 'And had it not been for your mad Ludwig the Second there would have been no Wagner.'

Neither of these statements is wholly correct, of course. Bayreuth was a thriving, growing town long before the great composer went to live there. And Richard Wagner, had he not found a royal patron willing to finance and encourage him, would most certainly have acquired another wealthy sponsor in the course of time. In his more mature years he was as skilled at extracting money out of people as he was in writing music.

Wagner was not, as some people are inclined to believe, a native of Bayreuth or even a Bavarian. He was born in Leipzig on 22 May 1813, of such doubtful parentage that even he was never able to determine it with exactitude. It is alleged that his mother was a daughter of Prince Constantin of Weimar and that his father was a third-rate actor named Geyer, both of them being illegitimate, as was Wagner himself. He used the name of Geyer until he began to study music at Leipzig University in 1829, when he changed it to Wagner. One thing about him is certain and that is he was in no way related to Rudolf Wagner, the famous German anatomist and physiologist who was born in Bayreuth in 1805, although two of his biographers have claimed that he was.

There can also be no doubt that Wagner's nebulous background and his illegitimacy were contributory causes of his somewhat unbalanced attitude towards life. But he was mainly haunted by fear that he might have Jewish blood in his veins. He had been accused of this when a student and his immediate reaction had been to develop an intense hatred of Jewry. Many people do not realise that, besides being a prolific composer, he also wrote a number of books and tracts and nearly all of his writings show his fanatical anti-Semitism. He had also extremely reactionary political leanings and, in his earlier days, was forever getting himself into bad odour because of them.

Wagner's earlier efforts at composition were disastrous and most of these immature works were never publicly performed until after his death. He was constantly in debt, twice going to prison for it, and when he eventually succeeded in getting *Rienzi*, *The Flying Dutchman* and *Tannhäuser* played before a lukewarm audience in Dresden, he promptly went and blotted his copybook by becoming involved with revolutionary supporters of Karl Marx. After the attempt at revolution failed, he was compelled to flee first to Paris and then to Zurich, spending the next ten years of his life in exile and, once again, in abject poverty.

He was allowed to return to Germany in 1861, but met with little success until he went to Munich and secured the patronage of Ludwig II. The young and already feeble-minded king showered costly presents and large sums of money upon the composer, after which the sycophantic nobility fawned upon him and his works were received with great enthusiasm in the capital. Unfortunately he could not resist the temptation to meddle in politics again and he was forced to return to exile in Switzerland. In the meantime, he had formed an attachment to Cosima – the wife of von Bülow, his musical conductor and at one time his best friend – who subsequently left her husband and followed Wagner to Switzerland. Cosima, who was an illegitimate daughter of Franz Liszt, was divorced by von Bülow in 1870 and married Wagner shortly afterwards.

Wagner's second life in exile was not as impoverished as his first one had been. His close relationship with the monarch of Bavaria and his courtiers had invested him with an air of glamour and he put this to good use. He found many wealthy friends in Switzerland and interested them in his plans for building what he assured them would be the most magnificent opera house in the world. They subscribed liberally towards a fund for this purpose and also smoothed the path for his return to Bavaria in 1874. He chose Bayreuth as the site for his opera house and his ambition was finally achieved in 1876, mainly on credit.

Bayreuth then became Wagner's final permanent home, but he did not live long to enjoy it. Pressure of work and the onset of a nervous ailment began to undermine his strength and, whilst convalescing from a serious breakdown, he died of a heart attack in Venice on 13 February 1883. His opera house, now known as the Festival Theatre, lies a short distance from the centre of the town, surrounded by streets bearing the names of his most famous operas. It has perhaps better acoustics than any other similar building in the world and the performances now staged there by Wagner's direct descendants are truly superb, using the most modern techniques and lighting effects.

Wagner's old home, *Wahnfried*, lies towards the bottom of the street that bears his name, which runs south-east from the Sternplatz, the town's physical centre. The composer lies buried in the garden alongside his wife, who survived him by nearly half a century, dying at the age of 93 in 1930.

If solid proof should be needed that Bayreuth was a flourish-
ing, artistic town long before the advent of Richard Wagner,
it is to be found in the Margrave's Opera House, which lies just
off the Sternplatz. It is a magnificent example of rococo work
and operas were being performed there sixty years before
Wagner was born. Among those responsible for its construction
in 1745-48 were Carlo and Guiseppa Bibiena. The Bibienas were
a truly remarkable family, consisting of four generations of
theatre and scenery designers who were born in Italy during
the seventeenth and eighteenth centuries. Besides creating more
than a dozen different theatres in their native country, they
travelled all over Europe, leaving behind them a trail of opera
houses and theatres in Austria, Germany, France and Spain.
The Margrave's Opera House is generally considered to be their
greatest masterpiece. It was originally constructed as a private
theatre for the use of the Margravine Wilhelmine and her invited guests.

Also close to the Sternplatz, at the lower end of the Kanz-
leistrasse, you will find the parish church, with its imposing
Gothic choir and fine Renaissance altar-piece. And in the Ludwigstrasse lies the magnificent New Palace, once the residence
of the Margraves, with the Hofgarten beyond. Joseph Saint
Pierre, who also had a hand in building the Margrave's Opera
House, was responsible for the New Palace, which is vaguely
reminiscent of Buckingham Palace in its exterior appearance
and which now houses the Wagnerian Museum in its west wing.
It was built in 1753-4.

The Eremitage, summer residence of the Margraves, will be
found about five kilometres to the east of the town, on the other
side of the Autobahn. It is a fascinating place, consisting of two
separate palaces – one built by John David Rantz in 1715-18 and
the other by Joseph Saint Pierre in 1749-53 – with numerous
fountains and a large pleasure garden.

You will have realised by now that Bayreuth is a comparatively modern town, like those we have seen in Swabia and

10   *Bamberg: the Cathedral towers from the north-west*
11   *Bamberg: the 'Rider' in the Cathedral*

Franconia. Most of its historic buildings came into being during the eighteenth century and are in complete contrast with the medieval buildings of Augsburg and Bamberg. Indeed, the oldest structure now standing in Bayreuth is its Old Castle, again just off the Sternplatz, but even this was largely demolished by bombing. Still standing is its octagonal tower, dating back to 1600, which was originally a stronghold and a watchtower and formed part of the old palace occupied by the margraves of Brandenburg-Kulmbach. It is unique in that it has, in place of an orthodox stairway, a winding ramp to enable horses and ammunition to be taken to the top, some 25 metres above the ground. The Old Castle itself, now largely repaired, was reconstructed on the site of an older building by the French architect Charles Philippe Dieussant in 1691. Its church, built in 1753, contains some interesting stuccoes by the itinerant Italian artist Pedrozzi.

12   *Nürnberg: the clock on the Frauenkirche*
13   *Nürnberg: St Lorenz, with the 'Angel's Salutation' by Veit Stoss and the Tabernacle by Adam Kraft*

5. Bayreuth Interlude

On the afternoon of Wednesday, 12 January 1927, an important cremation took place in Bayreuth. Though the day was grey and bleak, with temperature near freezing point, it still did not deter many distinguished Germans from attending the ceremony. Had you been there, you would have seen Prince William of Hohenzollern (representing his father, the deposed Kaiser), King Ferdinand of Bulgaria, Prince Hohenlohe and Siegfried Wagner with his mother and other members of the Wagner family. And had you looked a little deeper into the crowd of some 300 mourners, you would have noticed a non-descript, shabby little man, wearing a trench coat and sporting a small black moustache, who was destined to become Reich Chancellor in only six years' time and to be hailed as the leader of his people in 1934.

At the funeral, the priest eulogised the dead man as 'a real Christian and a real German'. Yet in the plain oak coffin soon to be consigned to the flames were the remains of one who had been born an Englishman, of a family with a long tradition of loyal service to the English Crown.

How did he come to be here? And what is even more intriguing, how did he become one of Germany's most noteworthy citizens in the early twentieth century and the man who, in his later years, was very largely responsible for the rise of Adolph Hitler in his Third Reich?

Houston Stewart Chamberlain was born in Southsea, England,

on 9 September 1855. He was the third son of a distinguished naval officer, William Charles Chamberlain, who in turn was the third son of Sir Henry Chamberlain, first baronet, a former consul-general and chargé d'affaires in Brazil. Subsequently, William Charles was promoted to the rank of Rear-Admiral and became Admiral Superintendent of Devonport Dockyard.

Houston Chamberlain's mother also came from British naval stock. She was the only daughter of Captain Basil Hall, an officer with a fine service record who later achieved a certain amount of fame as a travel writer.

The two previous sons of the union were already growing into strapping youngsters but, unfortunately, Houston proved to be a disappointment almost from the day he was born. He suffered from various stomach and chest complaints and very nearly died at the age of five. Nevertheless, his father had decided upon a military career for the boy and, when still not in his teens, he was sent to the Lycée Imperiale at Versailles and, two years later, to Cheltenham College. There he was badly bullied as the result of not being able to take part in manly sports and, after less than two years, his health broke down again. He was placed under a German tutor, Otto Kuntze, and subsequently went to Geneva, where he studied natural sciences. He then went on to complete his education in Dresden and, whilst there, became absorbed not only in Richard Wagner's music but also in the composer's political writings.

During this period abroad, young Houston had been able support himself on a remittance from his father. It amounted to less than £5 a week but, in those days, it enabled him to live in comfort if not in mild luxury. Then, when the Rear-Admiral died in February 1878, the money stopped. His son wrote a number of begging letters to his brothers and sisters, but they declined to supply him with financial aid. For this they could not really be blamed, since his correspondence with his family during the past three years had shown him to have developed a passionate hatred for England and for all things English.

So he took the least line of resistance by marrying a German girl, Anna Horst, who was older than himself but was able to bring him a substantial dowry. Very little is known about his life with her thereafter though, from a book she published in 1923 (*Meine Erinnerrungen an Houston Stewart Chamberlain*), one gathers it was not a particularly happy marriage. She bore him no children and, indeed, he wrote later that his 'intercourse had been mainly with Germany'. But she did enable him to perfect his German, so that he was able to write and speak with extreme fluency in this, his adopted tongue.

Chamberlain was also fluent in French and his first literary works, discourses on Wagnerian operas, were published in this language. They met with no success whatsoever, so he decided to abandon writing and return to his natural science studies, attending lectures by Professor Weisner at Vienna University, where his fees were paid by Anna. He then fell ill again but, during his convalescence, he wrote and published *Recherches sur la sève ascendante* (Researches into Rising Sap), which brought him quite a lot of acclaim. Stimulated by this, he re-turned to Dresden and published his *Das Drama Richard Wagners* in 1892. This got off to a bad start, but became popular after Chamberlain brought out his life of Wagner in 1895. The latter was well-written, though much of it was founded on hearsay and too many pages were devoted to Wagner's views on Jewry.

Then, in 1899 he produced the book which really made him famous in political and sociological circles all over the world – his *Grundlagen des neunzehnten Jahrhunderts* (Foundations of the Nineteenth Century). It was a ponderous but scholarly piece of writing, full of anti-Semitism, and all devoted to the glorification of the German race, dividing the world into Teutons and anti-Teutons. In it Chamberlain stated: 'So long as there are true "Germanen" in the world, so long can and will we have confidence in the future of the human race.'

The book brought him warm praise from Kaiser William and,

what was far more important from Chamberlain's point of view, sold by the thousands throughout Europe. The floods of wealth and success that descended upon its author brought about a final rift in his relationship with Anna and not long after the turn of the century they were divorced.

It was in 1881 that he paid his first visit to Bayreuth to see Richard Wagner, with whom he had been conducting a desultory correspondence for the past five years. And he met for the first time the young girl who was to become his second wife. Indeed, Wagner's daughter, Eva, seems to have been wildly attracted to him from the word go although her mother, Cosima, later wrote of Chamberlain: '... a strange and ugly man with most disturbing eyes, like those of a madman. He seemed completely devoted to Richard and they spent many hours together in the garden, deep in conversation about I know not what ... he is dangerous, this Chamberlain, and I do not want him disturbing my Richard, who is far from well.'

With Anna out of the way and Richard Wagner dead, Chamberlain now returned to Bayreuth and, on 26 December 1908, he married Eva Wagner by special licence. There seems to have been a certain amount of opposition from the family, mainly on account of the fact that Chamberlain was nearly 25 years older than his bride, but Eva finally won the day. Cosima relented and actually permitted the couple to live at *Wahnfried* until they could find a suitable home of their own.

When the first World War broke out, Houston Chamberlain promptly sided with the Germans, although technically he was still a British citizen. He suffered interrogation and a short period of house arrest in consequence, but his marriage to Eva now stood him in good cause. The thought of anyone even dimly related to the illustrious composer being interned or forced to report to the police was anathema to the people of Bayreuth. So he was allowed to go where he pleased and he repaid the Germans for their tolerance by writing pamphlet after pamphlet of vicious anti-British propaganda. For this work he received the Iron Cross with white ribbon for non-combatants in April 1915.

The following July he contributed an article to the *North American Review* entitled 'England', which was a bitter and scurrilous attack on his mother country. On 9 September, his sixtieth birthday, one of his admirers declared that he was 'the most important German thinker and philosopher since Kant and Schopenhauer', which caused the *Frankfurter Zeitung* not only to rebuke him for daring to lecture the Germans on their duties, but also to take proceedings against him for libel. He lost the case and was fined 1,500 marks but, in August 1916, he was restored to his former stature by being naturalised with the full support of the Kaiser, the German High Command and the Town Council of Bayreuth.

He was then asked whether he would vary his propaganda and write pro-German leaflets in English. The idea was for them to be dropped from a Zeppelin over London and other strategic cities. There was nothing new about this conception, however, since leaflets had been dropped by German balloons over Paris during the siege of 1870. Chamberlain produced about half a dozen different pamphlets and some of them did actually find their way to London.

Immediately after the Armistice, he became interested in the revolutionary activities that were taking place in Munich and decided to visit the capital forthwith. He became embroiled in a number of heated arguments and, on one occasion, was slightly injured in a free fight after declaring that the reactionary elements were being financed by international Jewry.

Then in 1921, in an underground café on the Ludwigstrasse, he was introduced to Adolf Hitler, now a man of 32 years of age and an ardent nationalist. Hitler had read and studied *Die Grundlagen des XIX Jahrhunderts* as a young man and had been deeply interested by it, as he had been by the writings of Kant, Godineau and Wagner, who were three of his major idols. To find himself suddenly shoulder to shoulder with someone who was both the author of one of his favourite sociological works and also the son-in-law of his pet composer must have given his ego a great boost.

The two men met frequently after that and, when Hitler was imprisoned in the fortress of Landsberg, Chamberlain was given permission to see him on two occasions. Hitler's *Mein Kampf* was, of course, written at this time and anybody who has read it as well as Houston Chamberlain's main work will detect many similarities between the two. One thing is quite certain and that is that Chamberlain may not have actually sowed the seeds of anti-Semitism in Hitler's mind, but he undoubtedly forced them to germinate and grow.

Hitler visited and stayed with Chamberlain in Bayreuth twice during 1926, once for three days in the spring and again for more than a week in the late summer. His host was, in fact, ceremoniously enrolled as a member of the Nazi party exactly nine months before he died.

As I have already stated, Hitler attended Chamberlain's funeral, although he remained prudently in the background. But not very long afterwards he wrote a letter to Eva stating that, if her husband had lived, he would have become one of the founder-members of the new Reich. In his biography of Chamberlain, Alfred Rosenberg – one of the Nazi war criminals who was executed at Nürnberg – states almost the same words.

Houston Chamberlain's tomb is to be found in the Town Cemetery of Bayreuth, on the north side of the Erlangerstrasse, the beginning of the main road leading to Bamberg. It is only a short distance away from the tombs of Franz Liszt, Wagner's son Siegfried and the famous author, Jean Paul. Prior to the Second World War it was embellished with Nazi swastikas, but these have now been tactfully removed.

Finally, there is one curious incident that deserves mention. When Neville Chamberlain asked Hitler to meet him in Germany in 1938, the Führer went to great lengths to discover whether he was any relation to Houston. I understand that he was given an affirmative answer – although the connection, if any, must be extremely remote – after which he expressed himself highly delighted at having to treat with a 'cousin' of his one-time faithful friend and mentor.

Is it too much to presume that, had it not been for Houston Chamberlain, England might have been plunged into a bloody war before she had time to gird her loins?

14   *Weltenburg on the Danube: the Abbey*

6. Nürnberg

Every time I visit Nürnberg I find myself wondering what it must have been like to have lived there in the Middle Ages, when its inhabitants were disciplined more severely than in any other town in Bavaria or even in all Europe. I stand outside the old Town Hall, taking care to screen my eyes from the new shopping centre and the tops of the modern skyscraper blocks just visible on the horizon, and I think of the grim Lochgefängnisse beneath it, where countless offenders – even those who had committed petty misdemeanours – were imprisoned and tortured in the days of the Hohenstauffens, the despots who considered themselves to be second only to God.

And then I stroll across to the fabulously beautiful Schöner Brunnen in the centre of the Hauptmarkt and console myself with the thought that life in those hard times still had more than its full share of compensations. Only a man inspired by all the good things in the world could have carved those four tiers of delightful figures, surmounted by a delicate, elongated crown tapering off into a slender spire with a cross 20 metres above the ground. It would have been worth while being a browbeaten peasant just to enjoy the Schöner Brunnen and all the artistic profusion nearby.

Oppression is said to bring out the best in people and it undoubtedly did this in Nürnberg. Between the thirteenth and the eighteenth centuries, the town produced so many intellectuals, artists, musicians and skilled craftsmen that it would take a fair-

15 *Regensburg: the old town seen from the Steinerne Brücke*

sized volume to list them. It was the birthplace of the Minne-
singers – amongst whom was the great Tannhäuser – and it later
became the centre for the Mastersingers.

It is said that a medieval scholar, after travelling through
the whole of Germany, wrote in his diary that in Nürnberg he
had seen an entire world. I believe that contention still holds
good today. There is so much of the past to be admired, so much
of the present to be enjoyed, that it is not surprising to discover that the Nürnbergers seldom stray far afield. At a travel
agency in the town they told me recently that business was
nothing like as brisk as it was in their Augsburg, Würzburg and
Munich branches, despite the fact that Nürnberg now has a
population well over half a million and possesses its own airport
with regular scheduled services. 'The Nürnbergers don't seem
to want to leave their homes for more than a few days', I was
told. 'And when they do, they always come back complaining
about the places where they have been.'

Maybe this has given them a parochial attitude towards life,
but it's a nice, friendly attitude all the same. They are so much
in love with their city that they go to great lengths to show
it off to visitors. I cannot imagine any Londoner – nor even a
Parisian or a Roman – exhibiting so much enthusiasm for his
home town.

And yet old Nürnberg, once described as 'the treasure chest
of the German empire', is nothing like as ancient as it appears
to be at first sight. It is because it was mainly built at a time
when architects were great artists as well as superb craftsmen
that it delights the eye and gives the impression of antiquity.
There has been nothing to show that the Celts or Romans were
here, or even the early Christians. The town was probably
started at the beginning of the eleventh century and most of
the places of interest in the Altstadt were built between the
thirteenth and seventeenth centuries.

Before you take a look at these places, cast a quick eye over
the new town that has sprung up well outside of the city walls

and largely since the end of the war. You will observe how the modern buildings have been designed to contrast strikingly with the old yet, at the same time, harmonise with them perfectly. It is as if an age-old and valuable gem has been given a new setting. The town planners of Nürnberg are to be congratulated on this stroke of rare genius. Even the strictly industrial areas, where they produce everything from machine tools and chemicals to cuckoo clocks and children's toys, are a good deal less unsightly than most.

If you have a car and intend merely to pay a day visit, I strongly advise you to leave it in one of the parking places just outside of the city walls. Many of the streets in the Altstadt are narrow and one-way and there is not an abundance of car parks. In any case, the town is best explored on foot and there are plenty of buses should you get tired.

Nürnberg is another of those Bavarian towns whose old city wall is still virtually intact. Indeed, it is one of the most perfect specimens to be found anywhere today and certainly one of the largest. There are four magnificent towers at each of its four corners – the Läufertor (Messenger's Tower) in the north-east, the Königstor (King's Tower) in the south-east, the Spittlertor (Spittler's Tower) in the south-west and the Neutor (New Tower) in the north-west – each forming a main gateway. If you come to Nürnberg by train, you will see the Königstor immediately opposite the main railway station.

From this tower, the wide Königstrasse will lead you straight up to the Hauptmarkt in the centre of the town. On your way, you will pass the Protestant church of St Martha on your right. This for many years housed the Mastersingers. Then, a little farther up on your left, you will see the Mauthalle, a large fifteenth-century building once used as a granary. These granaries were of vital importance to the citizens of Nürnberg in medieval days, since they were the main sources of food in times of siege.

A little farther up, on the right, is the magnificent Protestant church of St Lorenz, built during the thirteenth and fourteenth centuries. It contains the renowned Hail Mary Statue by Veit Stoss (1519), a late Gothic tabernacle by Adam Kraft and a wooden crucifix also by Veit Stoss, as well as a wealth of extremely valuable stained glass. Almost directly opposite, where the road is joined by the Karolinenstrasse and then bends slightly to the right, you will see the sixteenth-century Nassauerhaus, now forming a part of the main shopping centre.

As you enter the Haupmarkt, your eyes will be caught by the sheer beauty of the Schönen Brunnen, which I have already described. The word *Brunnen* means a fountain and crystal clear water still spouts from the figures of the six Cardinal Virtues, as it has done for nearly 600 years. Before you get to the Schönen Brunnen, take a look at the Frauenkirche on your right. The wonderful exterior clock is equipped with a number of gilded figures which, every day at noon, process in front of the figure of the Emperor Charles IV and do obeisance to him. If I remember rightly, the figures – in order of precedence – are those of the King of Bohemia, the Count Palatine, the Margrave of Brandenburg-Kulmbach, the Duke of Saxony and the Archbishops of Trier, Cologne and Mainz. Their quaint little performance is referred to as the Männleinlaufen, which may be translated as the Mannikins' Parade. The Frauenkirche, built in 1355-61, has three naves and two choirs and contains the Tucher Altar by Albrecht Dürer and two Epitaphs by Adam Kraft.

Above the Frauenkirche is the Old Town Hall, containing the dungeons and torture chamber I mentioned earlier on, which may be inspected by the public during the summer season, normally between 1000 and 1600 hours from Monday to Fridays between ten and one o'clock on Saturdays and Sundays.

And now we come to the church of St Sebaldus, a large and imposing building situated at the north of the Hauptmarkt with its main entrance in nearby Weinmarkt. This has sometimes been referred to as Nürnberg Cathedral, but it is a complete misnomer, because the town it not and never has been a bishop's see. Indeed, Nürnberg has been for long a bastion of Protestant-ism and the prince-bishops who ruled throughout Bavaria in bygone days were all of Catholic persuasion. St Sebaldus, which also possesses three naves and two choirs, was consecrated as a Catholic church in 1273 and became Protestant in the six-teenth century. Inside it are works by Veit Stoss and Adam Kraft and its most interesting feature is the tomb of St Sebaldus by Peter Vischer. Like the church of St Lorenz, it also has some priceless stained glass.

Do not be surprised if you find a political or religious meet-ing taking place in the Hauptmarkt. The place is Nürnberg's counterpart of Hyde Park's 'Speaker's Corner' and all sorts of fanatics gather there to air their grievances and propound their strange theories. But I like the Hauptmarkt best in December, when snow is on the ground and the traditional Christkindles-markt (Christmas Fair) is in progress. With its illuminations, its gay, colourful stalls, its carol singers and the bells of its churches pealing merrily through the cold night air, it is an experience never to be forgotten.

If you walk across the Weinmarkt, you will find the Albrecht Dürer house almost facing you. This is a beautifully preserved Gothic building dating back to 1450 in which the great artist lived from 1509 till his death in 1528 and it now contains a rich collection of his original drawings and engravings, to-gether with copies of his more famous pictures. A memorial to Dürer stands outside.

Overshadowing the Dürer house and not far from it is the Kaiserburg – the Emperor's Castle – which, in fact, forms a part of the city's north wall. It is alleged to be the oldest of all Nürnberg's buildings, although I have been unable to find any precise date for its foundation and the local records concerning its origin are ambiguous if not downright misleading. Possibly a key to the mystery lies in the castle's well (Tiefer Brunnen) which, so I am assured, has been a source of drinking water since the middle of the eleventh century. The Kaiserburg was for long the residence of the ruling Hohenstauffens and relics of their past occupation are still to be seen in the magnificent Emperors' and Knights' Halls and the romanesque double chapel. The Imperial Stables, to the east of the castle, have now been converted into a youth hostel. Walking past them will bring you to the Tetzeigasse in which lies the City Library, containing Nürnberg's archives, with the Apollo Fountain in front of it.

Crossing the road at the lower end of the Tetzeigasse will bring you to a street that runs down behind the Town Hall and the Frauenkirche to the Hans Sachs monument and the river.

Nearly all of Bavaria's major towns are strategically built on rivers, since they were a valuable means of transport in the Middle Ages. The river passing through Nürnberg is the Pegnitz, not to be confused with the Regnitz of which it is a tributary. It rises in the highlands near Bayreuth and winds its way southwards for about 100 kilometres to join the Regnitz canal system just west of Nürnberg. Large barges can travel comfortably down its lower reaches.

Lying athwart the river just below the Frauenkirche is the Heilig Geist Spital, once an almshouse run by a holy order and now incorporating a *weinstube* where you can enjoy fine food and wines. If you now follow the river westwards, passing the Hauptmarkt on your right, you will come first to the Karlsbrücke and then to a carefully preserved wooden bridge which dates back to the fourteenth century. This is the Henkersteg (Hangman's Walk) and it leads to a small island upon which the public executioner lived in solitary seclusion from the citizens. To the north of it lies the Weinstadel, a warehouse where they once stored grains and wines, together with the old water tower. And on the south bank is a building called the Umschlitthaus. Translated literally, this means 'the turnover house', referring to the fact that the place was once used by merchants for clearing their produce.

Taking one of the streets facing the Umschlitthaus will lead you down to a quiet little backwater where you will find another old water tower – one of the tallest buildings in the town, the Catholic church of St Elizabeth and the Protestant church of St James. The area around here is liberally endowed with old fountains and memorials, including the fine Peter Henlein Fountain, which stands in the Hefnersplatz.

There still remains a host of minor antiquities to be seen in Nürnberg, but I feel it is now time for us to turn our attention to some of the more modern places of interest. As may well be imagined, most of these lie outside the city wall, although you will find a few of them, such as the Industrial and Natural History Museums, the City Art Gallery and the Economics and Social Science faculties of the University, in the region south of the river between St Lorenz church and the east wall. But first and foremost comes the Städtbühnen in the Richard Wagner Platz, just off the Frauentorgraben and a short distance to the west of the railway station. This is a sort of respelendent art centre, embodying two theatres and an opera house. Wagnerian operas are performed here regularly, as are plays by Ibsen, Brecht and Shakespeare.

A little farther west, in the Lessingstrasse, is the Verkehrsmuseum (Transport Museum) which contains a breathtaking collection of original railway vehicles, including the first German train, a fine model railway and, curiously enough, a valuable collection of postage stamps. It is a veritable paradise for children and most parents will find it a difficult task trying to drag their offspring away!

On the south side of the station is the Meistersingerhalle, built rather after the style of London's Festival Hall, which has now become one of the most important centres of musical entertainment in Germany, staging performances by many of the world's leading orchestras. It is only a short distance away from the Academy of Fine Arts which, in turn, is just across the railway from the Tiergarten with its modest but excellent zoo.

Whilst on the subject of entertainment, I should mention the International Organ Week, held every June with virtuosos coming from all over Europe; the Kaiserburg Concerts, recitals by candlelight held throughout the summer in the castle halls; the summer evening concerts staged in the Heilig Geist Spital; the Hans Sachs plays performed by strollers in the streets of the old town; and, of course, the world-famous International Toy Fair, which takes place every February. On warm June and July evenings, you will also discover serenading going on in some of the historical courtyards.

There is, in fact, practically no limit to the enjoyment to be found in this old city. And to make your pleasure complete, the Nürnbergers can offer you some of the finest wines and the tastiest food to be found anywhere on the Continent. Their great speciality is, without doubt, their *Bratwürste*, small grilled sausages with a delightful flavour that are usually served up on pewter plates. Go to Bohm's in the Rathausgasse or the Sebaldus-Stuben in the Albrecht-Dürer Platz if you want to try them at their best. And make a special point of sampling the *Schnitzel* in the Nassauerkeller (beneath the Nassauer Haus and the *Herrentopf* in Bohm's Herrenkeller on the Theatre-strasse. But don't blame me if you start putting on weight!

There is one little tip I would like to pass on with respect to food. Restaurants such as the ones I have mentioned above are inclined to be a bit expensive. But do not despair. If you intend to stay in Nürnberg for any length of time and do not wish to burn a hole in your pocket, explore some of the little *bier-stuben* that lie just within the city walls. You will find that most of them are able to offer excellent fare at very reasonable prices. Only recently, I found the best gammon that I have ever tasted in a tiny place close to the Halletor. It cost me less than three marks! As for inexpensive hotels, I would recommend the Laurentius-Klause, not far from the Henkersteg, for anybody's money.

Finally, I cannot conclude this chapter on Nürnberg without some reference to the two great historical events which have occurred there in recent times, grim and tragic though they may have been.

On 15 September 1935 the Nazi leaders met in the town to execute a decree excluding all Jews from German citizenship. It was to foreshadow the greatest and most damnable massacre of all time.

Just over a decade later, on 20 November 1945, some of those self-same leaders together with many others were brought to trial in Nürnberg on a charge of committing war crimes. Three were acquitted, most of the others were given various terms of imprisonment, but 12 were sentenced to death by judicial hanging and ten died in this manner on 16 October 1946. Of the other two, one ended his life by suicide and the other, tried and sentenced in his absence, has never been seen since.

I like to think that this trial was held in Nürnberg because of what happened there in September 1935, although I have never seen any written evidence to support this theory. Whether the hangings were completely justified or whether, as many devout Christians have since maintained, it was an act of pure barbarism, only posterity can decide. All I can state with complete conviction is that the older people of Nürnberg, who were never entirely won over by the Nazi movement, are trying desperately to forget this unsavoury episode in their history. And the younger people, bless their hearts, have been brought up and educated in a more enlightened spirit and age.

7. Regensburg and the Enchanted Forest

The Danube, never a predictable river at the best of times, behaves in a very curious manner after crossing the Bavarian border at Ulm. One would have expected it to take the shortest and easiest possible course towards the sea but, instead, it appears to go uphill, flowing in a north-westerly direction and, after twisting and turning for nearly 250 kilometres, reaches its most northerly point almost exactly on the forty-ninth parallel. It is here that you will find the city and inland port of Regensburg, where vessels of well over 1,000 tons can ply the waters without difficulty.

About 25 kilometres before it gets to Regensburg and at a point where it is joined by its tributary, the Altmühl, the Danube reaches Kelheim, with a magnificent gorge nearby. It is here that you will find what I call one of Bavaria's freaks – a somewhat garish rotunda in Greco-Roman style called the *Befreiungshalle*, which was built in 1842-63 by Klenze and Gärtner to commemorate the Wars of Liberation against Napoleon. It is not for me to pass judgment on it here, so I can only repeat that, at the beginning of this century, it was described by a famous British architect as one of the Seven *Blunders* of the World. The same gentleman also included in his list the Walhala Hall of Fame, another of Klenze's efforts, which lies on the Danube to the east of Regensburg.

However, Kelheim is well worth a visit, if only to see the delightful Benedictine monastery at nearby Weltenburg, which actually dates back to A.D. 612 and which has a fine baroque church dedicated to St George and built early in the eighteenth century by the brothers Asam. In my opinion, the best way of reaching Kelheim is by motorboat from Regensburg. The journey takes the best part of two hours, but you will enjoy every minute of it and get a magnificent view of the gorge en route.

As for Regensburg itself, I am going to stick my neck out and say that I consider it to be one of the finest examples of an unspoilt medieval town in the whole of Western Europe. If I had to advise a tourist with only one day to spend in Bavaria which town he should see, I would unhesitatingly recommend Regensburg because, to my mind, it is the quintessence of all Bavarian history, tradition, architecture and way of life.

For one thing, it is probably the oldest civilised settlement in the entire Free State, though no one can say for certain just who were the first peoples to make their homes here. But we do know beyond any shadow of a doubt that the Romans found a large thriving Celtic community on the spot when they arrived more than 2,000 years ago. The place was then named Radasbona and the large fortress that the Romans erected on the site was called Castra Regina. It was subsequently ravaged by the Marcomanni during one of their frequent incursions into Roman-held territory and then, in A.D. 179, it was rebuilt and heavily refortified by the troops of Marcus Aurelius. After his death the following year, his son Commodus made peace with the Marcomanni, who retired to Bohemia and finally returned to Bavaria as friendly settlers during the sixth century. By that time, the Romans had been ousted for good and Castra Regina had become the seat of Bavarian dukes, who had renamed it Regensburg or, more accurately, Reganesburg.

Regensburg was for many years a free city. You will have come across this expression in connection with other Bavarian towns and I feel the time has come to explain it, in case the reader may not fully understand its significance.

Germany, unlike France or Britain, was until comparatively recently very much a land divided, largely due to the incessant squabbling that occurred amongst its hierarchy. For centuries the country was overrun by so many kings, princelings, dukes, margraves, landgraves and barons that the student of German history might well find himself wondering whether any commoners actually existed. A great number of these titles did not result from any royal decree or warrant, but were assumed by landgrabbers on a sort of sliding scale principle, the importance of the title depending upon the amount of land that had been grabbed. You appropriated a few thousand acres, browbeat the peasants into building you a castle and called yourself a landgrave, and nobody dared to say nay.

After a large part of Germany became absorbed in Charlemagne's empire, the country was dominated by the Carlovingians for about a century. Then, in 916, it became an independent monarchy for the first time, when Duke Conrad I was elected king. But there still remained a number of noblemen who persistently rebelled against the sovereign and who continued to do so for more than three centuries whilst the throne was occupied by a succession of Guelphs and Hohenstauffens. By the time the latter house went into decline in 1254, Germany was divided into some 275 different states, many of whose rulers were now insisting upon their right to elect any future kings.

Not all of these states were openly hostile towards a single, omnipotent monarchy. A number of them were German towns which had been granted their autonomy by a face-saving imperial charter, giving them all the prerogatives of a principality or duchy and the right to be represented in the German Diet in very much the same way as an English parliamentary constituency has the right to send a member to Westminster. These towns were known as 'imperial free cities' and some of them, including Augsburg, Nürnberg and Ulm, grew so great in importance that they came to be regarded as small, independent realms and were ruled by a prince-bishop, a duke or a margrave. Not to be outdone, many other German cities declared them-selves to be 'free' without the official sanction of the king-emperor and also became autonomous, although they were not such a power in the land as their imperial counterparts.

Thus all the free cities were, in fact, separate entities. At the same time, they still theoretically owed allegiance to the King-Emperor and the imperial free cities had a say in his election. They remained politically powerful until the fifteenth century, after which they became slowly absorbed into their respective territorial states until only six remained – Augsburg, Bremen, Frankfurt, Hamburg, Lübeck and Nürnberg. These, too, were destined to lose their autonomy in the course of time although they still retain the courtesy title of Freistadt.

Regensburg was proclaimed an imperial free city in 1245 and remained a dominant power in Germany for a little over two centuries. It had been a permanent episcopal see since 759 and the Roman Catholic Church thereafter continued to main-tain a strict control over its inhabitants for nearly 800 years. But, in 1541, the first of two historical Interim Diets met in the city. This, like the second Interim Diet which followed in Augs-burg in 1548, was an attempt to establish a joint Protestant and Roman Catholic council in order to reach a form of agreement between both parties. It was, in effect, the first serious attempt to settle the differences between the two churches and was largely inspired by the preachings of Martin Luther. And, in Regensburg, it produced a curious result. The whole town coun-cil and most of the more important citizens turned Protestant, whilst the clergy and by far the large proportion of the popula-tion remained steadfastly Catholic!

This schism was to mark the end of Regensburg's erstwhile greatness but, at the time of the Thirty Years' War, it regained much of its original prestige by becoming the official seat of the German Reichstag. Deliberations in this parliament were so long and protracted that it became known as the 'Everlasting

Diet,' a contemporary German version of our own Long and Rump Parliaments only on a much more tedious scale! The armistice between France and Austria was signed in Regensburg in 1684 and the Reichstag continued to sit in the town until 1806, four years before the city lost its last remaining vestiges of autonomy and became absorbed in the new Kingdom of Bavaria.

Regensburg's last official ruler, from 1803 until 1810, was Karl Theodor von Dalberg, a prince-bishop of Mainz and a close friend of both Goethe and Schiller. He was a well-loved, scholarly man, but he made a grave error in siding with Napoleon, who created him primate of the ill-starred and short-lived Rhine Federation. It is interesting to note that the last heiress of the von Dalberg family married in 1832 the English baronet Sir Ferdinand Acton, who thereafter added the name of Dalberg to his own surname. Their son, who became the first Baron Acton, was yet another of the leading figures who have tried to unite Protestants and Catholics in a common communion and one wonders whether he was inspired in this by his Bavarian ancestry.

Several recent chroniclers of Regensburg's history have stated that it sank into oblivion at the beginning of the twentieth century. This I refuse to accept, as I feel sure you will once you have visited the city. It is today a quiet, dignified place, not unlike one of the older English cathedral towns, but it is full of vitality and its 150,000 inhabitants, most of whom derive their incomes from making pottery, furniture, electronic equipment and musical instruments, are some of the nicest people in all Europe. Regensburg is still a bishop's see and the seat of a local government. And, most important of all, it is the home of the world-renowned *Domspatzen*, the finest cathedral boys' choir to be found anywhere.

There is one other point to which I should refer before we take a look at the town's treasures. Regensburg is also widely known by its alternative name of Ratisbon – indeed some of its own guidebooks actually prefer to describe it as such. It is a name that dates back to the Celtic Radasbona, that was resuscitated during the French occupation and of which many Regensburgers are inordinately proud.

Let us begin our tour in the Alter Kornmarkt, which lies exactly where the inner fortifications of the Roman camp stood in A.D. 200. To the north-west of this you will see the Roman Tower, St Ulric's Church and the Ducal Court. The tower, although it still displays a quantity of Roman masonry, is mainly of Caroline origin, and the Court, raised on the site of the old Praetorium was built c. 1200 and became the residence of the Bavarian dukes known as the Agilofingers. Pay special attention to the romanesque windows, then go inside and take a look at the Duke's Hall on the first floor. This was where justice was dispensed in the thirteenth century. The church of St Ulric is of more recent date, having been built in the romanesque-Gothic transition period.

At the south-west corner of the Kornmarkt lies the Old Chapel, which may well be one of the earliest Christian foundations in Europe. It was first raised by the Agilofingers and then rebuilt by Ludwig the German during the ninth century, using stones taken from the nearby Roman walls. It was restored, remodelled and enlarged to the order of the Holy Roman Emperor Henry II in 1008 and the raised east choir was added in 1441. Part of the interior was given a rococo style decor in 1748. In its Chapel of Grace you will find the oldest known image of the Virgin Mary in Bavaria and one of the oldest in Germany.

The Kornmarkt and the whole of the old town are dominated by St Peter's Cathedral, considered by many experts to be a masterpiece of Gothic art and certainly the principal Gothic building in all Southern Germany. It was begun in 1275 on the site of a previous ecclesiastical building of which one part still remains. This has been quaintly named the Eselsturm or 'Donkey's Tower', though no one seems to know exactly how it acquired this somewhat unfortunate appellation. The twin towers and western façade of the cathedral were added in the fifteenth century, the former being completed in the nineteenth century by the addition of steeples, which were repaired and renovated in 1955. In the nineteenth century, too, much of the baroque interior decoration was taken away, leaving only the high altar in this style. The side altars in the north nave are Gothic and the stained glass windows are outstanding examples of fourteenth-century craftsmanship. On the two westernmost pillars is the fine Annunciation Group by the Erminald Master dating back to 1280.

The name *Domspatzen* actually means 'cathedral sparrows' but, although the boys take part in services in St Peter's, they are normally to be heard in St Ulric's, which is regarded as the choir church. Their recitals are pretty frequent and you should make a point of hearing them.

Adjoining the cathedral are the All Saints Chapel and St Stephan's Church. The former became the burial place of Regensburg's bishops in the mid-twelfth century and the latter, of Caroline origin, was for some time used by the bishops and canons for private prayer. Both buildings are of romanesque origin and are connected to the cathedral by a cloistered court-yard.

Directly north of the cathedral and halfway between it and the river stands the Porta Praetoria in the middle of a narrow street. It served as the north gateway to Castra Regina and is in remarkably good condition considering it has stood here since A.D. 179. Around it, as in other parts of the old town, you will see remains of the original fortifications, which enclosed a space about four times the size of London's Trafalgar Square.

Proceeding westward from this point you will come to a whole cluster of buildings that all belong to the thirteenth and fourteenth centuries – the castles and residences of Regensburg's former leading citizens. Unfortunately only about 20 of the original 60 still stand, but there are still enough to show the

16   *Schloss Herrenchiemsee: the Mirror Gallery*

opulent life that these people lived in medieval times. Note particularly the Haus an der Heuport, directly opposite the west door of the cathedral on the corner of the Kramgasse, the Goliathhaus, the Baumburgerturm and finally the Goldener Turm, which has nine floors and is believed to be the loftiest patrician castle still in a state of perfect preservation. The Goliathhaus, incidentally, received its name from the gigantic fresco covering its walls.

If you take the street opposite the Golden Tower and a little to the north of it, it will lead you into the Haidplatz with the Haus Zur Neuen Waag (New Weighhouse) on your right. I am not sure when it ceased the function for which it was built, but it certainly became a place for much weighty discussion in later years, when it was converted into a 'drinking parlour for gentlemen'. It was the favourite haunt of Johann von Eck, a stern and ardent opponent of the Reformation during the first half of the sixteenth century, and it is said that two learned theologians actually fought a duel here on one occasion over the respective merits of Catholicism and Protestantism!

On the other side of the square stands the Haus Zum Goldenen Kreuz (Golden Cross Hotel) which, originally built as a private residence, later became a sumptuous inn where visiting royalty stayed during the course of three centuries. On the front of this building is a monument to Don Juan of Austria, hero of the battle of Lepanto, who was the illegitimate off-spring of the great Emperor Charles v and a Regensburg woman named Barbara Blomberg. It is said that Charles first met his future mistress when staying at the hotel.

A short distance to the north-east stands Regensburg's imposing Old Town Hall, facing the one-time cabbage market and distinguished by its Town Tower and Emperor's Balcony. It was mainly built between the fourteenth and sixteenth centuries and its magnificent Reichssaal, with its costly decorations and beautiful timbered ceiling, was for some time used by the citizens for festivities. It was here that the German Diet later

17 *Munich: Der Alte Peter seen from the Viktualienmarkt*

came to roost, as the pew-like benches and canopied chair of the Imperial Commissioner continue to bear witness. Other rooms in the building, some used by the Prince Electors and some as courts of law, remain virtually unchanged from the old days, although several of them now house the Diet Museum.

If your spine was chilled by the dungeons and torture chamber in Nürnberg, it will be frozen solid by the sinister, dimly-lit Fragstatt (Inquisition Room) in the basement of the Old Town Hall. In one portion of it – the Folterkammer – they have gone to the trouble of preserving all the foul instruments of torture in their original state and surroundings and, as you enter the evil place, your mind conjures up a vision of the cowled inquisitor seated at his desk and watching the reactions of his victim through a screen like that of a confessional.

With what devilish ingenuity did those medieval tormentors devise their infernal machines! There is a delightful contraption known as the 'Spanish Donkey', which has a spine as sharp as a knife edge. The victim was suspended from the ceiling and repeatedly drooped astride this 'animal' until his genitals were destroyed and he was eventually split asunder. Then there is another charming little contrivance affectionately called the 'Maiden's Lap', which has a seat composed of sharp wooden spikes. You sat your man down on it and piled weights on him until the points penetrated deep into his thighs and buttocks and he screamed aloud in agony. There is also a *strappado*, a triangle on which the victim was drawn upwards by his chin and neck and then dropped violently just clear of the floor, and a liberal assortment of whips, racks and thumbscrews. It is said that the so-called sophisticated methods of torture still used by some unenlightened countries in this modern world are much more effective but, after seeing Regensburg's Folterkammer, I can hardly believe it.

Returning to the cathedral and turning north will bring you to the Danube and to the Steinerne Brücke, the oldest practicable stone bridge in all Germany and the first ever to span the

Danube. Although it was built between 1135 and 1146, it has a remarkably modern appearance and is held to be one of the foremost examples of medieval skill left in the world today. As you cross it, you will observe that there are two islands in midstream, joined by another bridge which passes below you. The one on your right stands at a point where the river Regen joins the Danube and is where you go for the pleasure boats. Below you, also, you will see the remains of the Eiserne Steg which was the original ford across the river. It was at this point that the Romans built their port.

You can get a fine view of the old town from the north end of the Steinerne Brücke, and if you go a little farther, into the modern suburb of Stadttamhof, and climb the hill to the Dultplatz, you will be rewarded by a superb panorama of the entire city. I think you will be amazed to notice how a place of this size, in spite of its many new factories and increasing industrial activities, manages to retain a green belt that comes to within so short a distance of its centre.

Let us now explore that part of Regensburg that lies south of the cathedral, beginning with the New Parish Church which stands in the centre of the Neupfarrplatz, at the bottom of the Residenzstrasse. Its name always causes me some amusement, since it has been standing here for nearly 450 years, but the adjective 'new' refers to the fact that it was the first church to be built after the first Interim Diet. The site on which it stands was originally the city ghetto which, like the one in Bamberg, was destroyed when the Jews were expelled at the beginning of the sixteenth century. The church has been Protestant for most of its lifetime, although Catholic services were held in it during the first five years after it was opened.

There now remain three places of outstanding interest that should not be missed. Two of them lie close together at the southernmost part of the old town and may be approached by turning west out of the Neupfarrplatz into the Obere Bachgasse, walking down this and taking the third main turning on your right. This will bring you into the Emmeramsplatz and thus to the church of St Emmeram, which many people declare to be the oldest Christian building in Regensburg, despite the claims of the Old Chapel by the cathedral.

It seems almost incredible to realise that much of this church has been standing here for over 1,100 years and that its original foundations date back even farther, some say to the middle of the sixth century. It started its really active life as a Benedictine monastery in A.D. 820, though monks had settled here at least 100 years previously, and the building was erected over the grave of St Emmeram, one of the original missionaries who Christianised Bavaria. Another great patriarch, St Wolfgang, also came here in the tenth century, bringing fame to the church as a seat of culture and learning. He, too, lies beneath it in the crypt that bears his name. Close by is the tomb of St Hemma, queen of Ludwig the German, which was built in 1280 and is undoubtedly another masterpiece of Gothic art. St Emmeram's possesses two more crypts – the Ramwold Crypt, going back to 980 and the oldest church in Germany without aisles, and the Ring Crypt, in which stands the tomb of St Emmeram himself.

The interior of the church was decorated in baroque style by the Asam brothers in 1730 and the main porch displays the first architectural sculptures in Bavaria, believed to have been executed in 1050.

The Princes of Thurn and Taxis, who had originally occupied the twelfth-century Prüfening Benedictine monastery west of the city, moved into the Abbey of St Emmeram after the secularisation, incorporating the cloisters in their more modern castle (1748) which lies immediately behind the church. These princes were the hereditary principal commissioners of Regensburg, in other words they represented the King-Emperor in the Diet. Their burial vault is in the cloisters and the castle now houses the Marstall Museum.

The third building you should inspect is the church of St

Jakob, if only to gaze with awe at the amazing collection of romanesque sculptures over and around its main porch. As one local guidebook succinctly puts it, here indeed is a place where pagan and Christian traditions meet. And, I might add, meet in perfect harmony. St Jakob's was built round about 1200 and is often referred to as St James's *Scots* Church. This is something of a misnomer, because the missionaries who founded the original monastery on the site came not from Scotland but from Ireland. I think perhaps – and this is pure conjecture – there may possibly be some connection with Duns Scotus, the thirteenth-century Scottish-born Franciscan friar and doctrinal opponent of Thomas Aquinas, some of whose followers are known to have occupied the monastery *c.* 1350.

Regensburg is sometimes called the Gateway to the Bayerischer Wald and it is certainly a convenient centre from which to explore the forest. If you do not have a car, there are frequent motorcoach excursions in the summer as well as specially organised trips by train. But the real 'gateways', if such there be, are undoubtedly Amberg in the north and Deggendorf in the south and I propose now to take you on a circular tour of the Bayerischer Wald from one to the other.

Amberg, a town of some 50,000 inhabitants, is not unlike Rothenburg ob der Tauber in many respects and I believe it frequently refers to itself as the 'Oberpfalz Rothenburg'. It lies about 70 kilometres (44 miles) to the north of Regensburg by road and 60 kilometres (38 miles) east of Nürnberg. Like Rothenburg, it has preserved its old city walls, but its buildings, although of considerable interest, do not date so far back, the oldest of them being the Gothic Town Hall, constructed in 1336. It has a great many churches, those well worth seeing being St George's, built in 1370, and the unique Deutsche Schulkirche, designed by one of the Dientzenhofer brothers at the end of the seventeenth century.

Leading eastward out of Amberg is one of the main roads to Pilsen, in Czechoslovakia, and if we follow this for a short distance it will lead us to the edge of the Bayerischer Wald, with its wooded hills and mountains rising high in the distance.

Besides being the largest continuous forest area in Central Europe, the Bayerischer Wald has long been a source of inspiration for novelists and poets. In the German language Goethe and Schiller have extolled its virtues and several hundred romances have been written with the forest as a background. It still remains an idyllic paradise for the most part, but I should warn you that it is one of those places that should best be explored on foot. If you go hurtling through it in a car, you will miss 90 per cent of its beauty, whereas a train journey will take you only to those towns which, like the ones on the Romantic Road, have suffered badly from commercialisation.

My father, who could *walk* the hindlegs off a mule, took me hiking through the Bayerischer Wald when I was a boy of 13 and I can remember it vividly to this day. I retired to bed in some small inn completely exhausted each night, but I covered no less than 250 miles in the space of sixteen days and I sincerely believe that the exercise was largely responsible for the wonderfully good health I have enjoyed ever since. Father was then himself 59 years of age, but the clean, pine-scented air and the good, plain food we enjoyed at our various lodgings soon made him as fit and active as a man 30 years his junior.

To most Englishmen, the name of Adalbert Stifter will be unfamiliar. Yet, in the second half of the nineteenth century, he was as well known as an author to the peoples of Austria and Germany as Charles Dickens was to Londoners. One of his most popular works, *Aus dem bayerischen Wald*, has been translated into English and I strongly recommend any visitor to Bavaria to obtain a copy and read it from cover to cover.

Stifter, possibly because he was a sick man for most of his short life, was quick to realise that the forest was not only a place of great natural beauty but also an area possessed of unique health-restoring properties. In 1876 he wrote: '...the air in the higher regions, which are still covered by the forest, is purer, because it is always so at high altitudes, and it is made even fresher and more wholesome by the natural resins of the pine trees and by the breathing of their millions of leaves and needles, so that it will bring happiness and health like the water. And a person who has lost both happiness and health will get them back when he drinks the water and breathes the air. Moreover, not only health is restored; you will enjoy peace and an inner calm when you wander in these regions and absorb the surroundings.'

It all sounds rather like an old-fashioned advertisement for a patent medicine, but it is very true. I have known two cases of men given only a short time to live by their doctors who have gone to the Bayerischer Wald and made a complete recovery. And it is an indisputable fact that many of the inhabitants of this area suffer little by way of disease and live to a ripe old age. I can well remember meeting an old peasant just outside of Bodenmais not very long ago who proudly informed me that he had just attended the christening of his fifth great-great-grand-child. It subsequently transpired that he had four sons, 11 grandsons and 31 great-grandsons and that all of them were alive and well!

One usually associates health resorts in Germany with mineral waters and mud baths, but in the Bayerischer Wald they tend to specialise in what they call the *Luftkur* (air cure). Most of the places offering this form of treatment are at an altitude of about 2,000 feet above sea level and you have only to spend one or two nights there with your bedroom window open to find yourself revitalised by the atmosphere.

The Pilsen road will lead you through Wernberg and then, when you come close to the Czechoslovak border, you must turn sharply south and carry on for 56 kilometres (35 miles) to Waldmünchen. It is here that they stage the annual *Trenck*, a pageant to commemorate the time when the town was occupied by Baron Trenck and his dreaded Croatian *pandours* (mounted constabulary) in the eighteenth century. Only a few kilometres south of Waldmünchen, you will discover another pageant taking place during the second week of August. This is the celebrated *Drachenstich* (Dragon Sticking) in Furth im Wald, celebrating the final repulse of the Magyars many centuries ago. It consists of an elaborate fancy-dress procession, in which the majority of the inhabitants take part, followed by a fight between a knight and an enormous realistic dragon breathing fire and smoke.

Continuing southwards we soon come to Neukirchen bei Heilige Blut, a small town where a miracle is alleged to have taken place 500 years ago and which is still a favourite place for pilgrims. From here the road carries on to the air cure resort of Lam, passes the foot of the Osser mountain (1,260 metres) and arrives at Lohberg, which is the highest town in the forest and another noted health resort. From here you can get superb views, not only of the Bayerischer Wald itself but also of a wide stretch of Czechoslovakia. Eight kilometres south and only a little lower is Bayerisch-Eisenstein, a popular winter sport resort, lying midway between the Arber (1,470 metres), the forest's highest mountain, and the Falkenstein (1,310 metres). If you want to enjoy a really superb view of the neighbourhood, you can go to the top of the Arber by the Arber-Doppelsessellift chair lift, which will cost you about $2\frac{1}{2}$ marks for the return journey.

Not far from here the two heads of the river Regen have their sources and we now follow one of them down to Zwiesel. This has been for many centuries an important glass-making centre, and it is well worth while paying a brief visit to the works, if only to see the glassblowers practising some of the arts that seem to have been almost forgotten in this modern age. Zwiesel is also the venue for an annual International Wood Sawing Contest, when teams from all over Europe compete in sawing through massive tree trunks a metre or more in diameter. Naturally this is a thirst-making exercise and it is intriguing to watch competitors downing a litre of the local brew in only a few seconds before tackling the next trunk!

Now we come to Regen, the town where the two heads of the river join and which takes its name from the river proper. Here every summer they indulge in a magnificent junketing known as the Pilchsteiner Festival, followed by a roisterous Pilchsteiner Dinner to which all and sundry are invited. Here also are the ruins of Weissenstein Castle where, so the story goes, a certain Count Hund buried his wife alive because she drowned their baby in the river.

And so downstream for 32 kilometres (20 miles) to the other gateway, Deggendorf, where the Danube, the Isar and the Regen all meet. It is a fine old town, sadly underrated by most guidebook writers, which was founded about A.D. 750 and has a delightful sixteenth-century Rathaus. It also happens to be something of a curiosity, in that it is the only Old Town in Bavaria situated on the north bank of the Danube. You will also find a splendid prehistorical museum here – probably one of the best in Germany – and I strongly recommend it as a centre in which to stay, since its very best hotels offer board and lodging at remarkably low terms.

Not far north of Deggendorf and also on the Danube is Straubing, an extremely peaceful little town of about 40,000 inhabitants, which shows traces of Celtic and Roman occupation and boasts a fourteenth-century Town Tower, a fifteenth-century late Gothic 'hall-type' cathedral and a Carmelites' church containing some very old and valuable stained glass. It was here, in the year 1435, that Agnes Bernauer, a commoner who had married the only son of Duke Ernst of Bavaria, was condemned as a sorceress by her father-in-law and thrown into the Danube after being cruelly tortured. Her body now lies buried in the chapel dedicated to her in Straubing's church of St Peter, which also has a famous military cemetery.

I could go on writing forever about the Bayerischer Wald, its quaint towns and villages, its remarkable people and its wide diversity of pageants and festivals. But it is infinitely better for you to find out these things for yourself. The forest still remains largely unspoilt, thanks to the fact that it has not been too widely publicised, and it offers great opportunities to the explorer. By searching diligently, you will soon come across a place that you can keep to yourself, far from the madding crowds of tourism. And, having found it, be sure to keep it dark.

There are two little points of interest that I think I should mention before closing this chapter. Wherever you go in the forest, you will stumble across quaint boards by the roadside and on the walls of houses that bear inscriptions to the departed and look remarkably like gravestones. These are the *Totenbretter* (Dead Boards), which the people of the Bayerischer Wald erect in memory of their dear ones. They are purely memorials and do *not* mark any actual graves.

Secondly, do not be repulsed by the profusion of toadstools you will find, not only growing under the trees but being offered for sale in the village shops. Two species are real delicacies and infinitely preferable to the common or cultivated mushroom. The *boletus* – a large fungus which may be readily identified by its dark top and honeycomb-shaped gills – is the basis of nearly all mushroom soups sold in the shops today. The *chanterelle* – which is shaped like a trumpet, coloured orange-yellow and smells faintly like an apricot – has a delightful flavour and is my particular favourite of all edible fungi.

8. The Bavarian Tirol

As I have mentioned before, that part of Bavaria which the Germans call *Ober* or Upper is actually in the extreme south. It is very largely a mountainous region, although its highest peaks, whilst being more impressive than those in the Bayerischer Wald, are considerably lower than those to be found in the Swiss high Alps. On the other hand, many people find them more attractive. A lot of the mountains in Switzerland have a grim, almost hostile appearance, whereas their counterparts in Oberbayern are warm and friendly. In addition, most of them can be climbed with comparative ease, so that they afford a good training ground for budding alpinists.

In order to see as much of the country as possible, it is best to approach Oberbayern from Passau, a charming old town in the extreme south-east, where the large river Inn and the little river Ilz join the Danube just before it crosses the border into Austria.

I can never think of Passau without feeling a certain degree of embarrassment. In its fine fifteenth-century cathedral of St Stephen stands the largest organ in the world – a mighty monster with 211 stops and 17,000 pipes – and, many years ago, it caused me to make a fool of myself. I learnt to play the organ in my father's church and at Dulwich College when in my middle teens and, for a long time, I considered myself to be something of a virtuoso. But Passau put an end to that. I entered the cathedral one quiet summer's afternoon, found a little old sexton pottering around in the shadows and, after convincing him that I was no mean player, bribed the wretched fellow into opening up the organ for me and switching on the blower. Then, with all the confidence and aplomb of the man who found the lost chord, I sat down at the manuals, selected what I thought would make an excellent combination of stops and proceeded to play one of my favourite Mendelssohn pieces. The sounds that emerged from the instrument were absolutely nerve-shattering! I don't know to this day what mistake I made or how I managed to make it, but the blasts from the pipes were enough to raise the roof. I tried the beastly thing again and again but, before I could put matters right, I was tapped gently on the shoulder by a grave priest and informed that a service was just about to commence. I left the organ feeling bitterly humiliated and I became even more ashamed of myself when I realised there was no service after all. The priest had told a deliberate white lie in order to remove me.

The great German traveller, Baron Friedrich von Humboldt, described Passau as one of the seven most beautiful cities in the world and it is certainly an architectural gem. It was once an important Roman military camp – they called it Castra Batava – and it became a bishopric as early as A.D. 739. Around the cathedral, originally late Gothic but largely rebuilt in 1668-86, you will find some magnificent old houses, whilst in the square is the seventeenth–eighteenth-century baroque New Palace of the Prince-Bishops, which has a fine ceremonial staircase and a court theatre. Amongst the oldest buildings are St Severin's church, with its ninth-century main aisle and a notable statue of the Madonna (*c.* 1450), and the Niedenburg Monastery, now a girls' school, attached to the eighth-century Church of the Holy Cross. This contains the grave of the Abbess Gisela, sister of the Emperor Henry II and one-time wife of the first King of Hungary, St Stephen, after whom the cathedral is named.

Crossing the Danube by the Luitpoldbrücke, you will arrive at the thirteenth-century fortress of Oberhaus standing, like the fortress of Marienberg in Würzburg, on the summit of a small hill. It was for many centuries occupied by the Prince-Bishops before they moved to the New Palace and was altered and enlarged by them in successive reigns. It now houses an interesting little museum.

During July, Passau stages a festival of drama and music which I personally consider to be one of the best in all Bavaria. It is not as ambitious as those to be found in some of the larger cities, but it has a great charm all of its own.

Not far to the south-west of Passau is the small town of Fürstenzell, with its fine Monastery Church of the Assumption built in 1745, and then the road carries on past the thermal health resort of Bad Füssing-Safferstetten until it reaches Simbach on the river Inn. There is nothing of absorbing interest to be seen here and I only mention it because of its connection with Adolf Hitler, whose aunt and uncle lived here during the end of the nineteenth-century. Hitler himself was born just across the river, in the Austrian border town of Braunau, where his father – who actually changed his name from Schicklgrüber to Hitler some years before Adolf was born – carried on business as a jobbing builder and also had a share in a bakery. And, indeed, a few of Hitler's distant relatives still live here, though perhaps it would not be prudent to mention their surnames.

About 20 kilometres (13 miles) farther on is the delightful small medieval town of Burghausen, which was once a completely self-contained castle, the seat of the Dukes of Bavaria from 1255 to 1505 and of the Electors of Bavaria from 1505 to 1779. Its 1,000 metres of fortifications, the longest of their kind in Germany, have been standing for more than 1,000 years. Burghausen also stages its own particular annual festival, the *Meier Helmbrecht* in July and August, and its castle is beautifully floodlit during the summer weekends.

If you are visiting Burghausen, you must on no account miss seeing Altötting, which is only a short distance to the north-west. This has an eighth-century Holy Chapel, one of the ten oldest churches in Germany, containing a shrine of Our Lady to which pilgrims flock all the year round. But none the less noteworthy is the Gothic Parish and Pilgrimage Church, which also has ancient foundations and was rebuilt in 1499-1511. In its treasury is the *Goldenes Rössel*, made round about 1400 and a superb example of goldsmiths' craft. Though almost invariably dubbed the 'Golden Horse', its correct name is the Adoration of the Infant Jesus. Also in the church is the burial vault of Marshal Tilly and a remarkable mechanical Christmas crib, the only one of its kind I have ever seen.

Altötting reminded me of Lourdes the last time I went there. It was just after dusk in mid-July and, as I entered the little town from the direction of Munich, I encountered a long procession of pilgrims, all carrying flaming torches and chanting a solemn hymn as they wended their way slowly to the Holy Chapel. On such occasions, even the most hardened agnostic may find himself wondering whether there might be something in Christianity after all. I will go further still and state that I consider Bavaria as a whole the perfect specific for agnosticism. It is almost impossible to feast your eyes upon so great a wealth of ecclesiastical architecture without becoming a believer.

Travel south from Altötting for 40 kilometres (25 miles) and you will come to the Chiemsee, the largest lake in the country and frequently referred to as the Lake of Bavaria. It is not very big in fact – not more than 19 kilometres long and 15 kilometres wide – but it is incredibly beautiful, with its blue waters, wooded surroundings and backcloth of mountains. And it is the scene of the famous water festival on the Feast of Corpus Christi, a splendid sight never to be forgotten.

There are two islands on the lake, which may be visited by taking the regular boat service. The smaller of these, known as the Frauenchiemsee, is the focal point of the water festival, which starts from its Benedictine monastery. This was founded in A.D. 782 by Duke Tassilo, then later destroyed and rebuilt in the tenth century.

The larger island, the Herrenchiemsee, has two castles built upon it. The older one, formerly a monastery also inhabited by Benedictines, dates back to about 1680, although its foundations show evidence of a much earlier structure. The other castle, the renowned Schloss Herrenchiemsee, was the idea of Ludwig II and probably the most fantastic one he ever dreamed up. It is said to have cost over half a million pounds, which was a tremendous sum of money in those days, but it was never fully completed and poor Ludwig was only able to spend a few days there in 1885, not long before his tragic death. In its remarkable *Paradesaal* you will see another of his almost crazy notions, his Golden Bed, a comfortable couch that could also be used as a throne. And in the dining-room, where the large table stands on a lift that connects it with the kitchens below, there is an exceptional rarity – a huge chandelier made not from crystal glass but from Meissen china! In the summer weekends the castle is ablaze with candlelight, whilst concerts are held in the Mirror Gallery, an exact replica of the famous gallery in the Palace of Versailles. To stroll in the beautiful gardens after sundown with soft music filtering through the castle windows is another experience never to be forgotten.

Prien, the only town of any size on the lake, is a good place in which to stay, with a number of comfortable, very reasonably priced hotels and pensions, but you may prefer Traunstein, which is only a few kilometres to the east. This is a charming little market town of some 15,000 inhabitants, steeped in history and smiling with hospitality, which has recently achieved fame as a health resort, offering its visitors brine and mud baths as well as cold water Kneipp cures. The surrounding countryside is not particularly attractive but, all the same, Traunstein makes an excellent centre from which to explore the mountain district and I have tasted better food here than in any other part of the Bavarian Tirol. At Eastertide, the town stages its unique St George's Day ride, when splendidly accoutred horses and riders accompanied by the local clergy set out from the square to be ceremonially blessed at the church of Ettendorf.

From Traunstein it is a short journey through Siegsdorf and Eisenärtz to Ruhpolding, which lies at a height of about 700 metres in a small hollow almost entirely surrounded by mountains. It is best enjoyed in the early months of the year, when it is a lively and extremely pleasant winter sports centre, but it still has plenty to offer the summer visitor. You can climb to the summits of the Rauchsberg and Steinberg, either by foot or by cable railway (the latter taking no more than five minutes), and get wonderful views of the whole area. Or you can just potter about in the town itself, examining its various old buildings, including the twelfth-century pilgrimage church. There is an interesting little museum and children will delight in the 'fairy tale wood' and 'fairy tale mill'.

About 20 kilometres (13 miles) south-west of Ruhpolding lies the delightfully named Reit im Winkl, almost on the Austrian border. This is a really lovely little place of less than 3,000 inhabitants, rising from 700 to nearly 900 metres on a slope. Since the war it has been largely developed as a winter sports centre and I personally consider it to be one of the best ski-ing resorts in all Europe, particularly for those who are not over-ambitious. It gets more snow than any other place in Bavaria and, at the same time, it can boast well over the average share of sunshine.

Perhaps I should digress here to say something about winter sports in Bavaria as a whole. Since the age of ten I have spent a great many hours of my life on skis in five different European countries, but some of the best times I have ever had have been in the Bavarian Alps. You are not troubled by thousands of boisterous, over-enthusiastic devotees of the sport and, if you happen to be something of a rabbit, you do not have to suffer chaff or sneers from the experts. Moreover, you are never confronted by exhorbitant hotel bills and excessive charges for

18   *Passau: the Cathedral from the west*

cable railways and chair lifts. Bavaria is even cheaper than Austria in this respect and that takes a lot of beating!

Ski-ing, I am glad to say, is becoming increasingly popular, especially among the English, but many people are deterred from enjoying the sport by the high cost and by the difficulty in finding suitable slopes on which to learn and gain experience. Bavaria offers a solution to both these problems. Reit im Winkl, Ruhpolding and other resorts I shall be mentioning later on can provide excellent board and lodging for well under two pounds a day and a weekly season on a chair lift will cost you round about 30 marks. Finally, you should remember that the air fare from London to Munich and back is only about 15 per cent more than those between London and Switzerland.

Over to the east of Reit im Winkl lies one of Bavaria's most fashionable spas, Bad Reichenhall. It, too, is by way of being a centre for winter sports, but I do not recommend it. Nor, for that matter, can I work up any real enthusiasm about the place in general. It is so typically what the Edwardians used to call 'a watering place' and, in truth, there is rather a stale Edwardian air about the whole town. However, you might find it worth your while to take the cable car up to the Predigstuhl (Preacher's Chair) if only to revel in the magnificent view. But once having taken a look at Bad Reichenhall, you will probably prefer to carry straight on to Berchtesgaden.

When I first visited Berchtesgaden in the late 20s and early 30s, it was an absolutely charming old-world town, bristling with glorious lime trees and thronged, but not overcrowded, with gay, smiling tourists sipping cool drinks and wolfing down patisseries whilst sitting under the striped awnings of countless little cafés and *Bierstuben*. It was, indeed one of those places that I never failed to visit during my earlier trips to Bavaria.

I came back in 1938 and was shocked to the core. Hitler by now had established his 'summer residence' on the summit of the 1,600-metre Kehlstein nearby and Berchtesgaden was filled to bursting with his sycophantic Nazi admirers – screaming 'Heil

19 *Osterhofen, near Passau: the High Altar in the Convent Church*

Hitler' at each other across the crowded streets – whilst jack-booted army officers paraded, always in pairs, up and down the pavements, scowling at any tourist who had the slightest sus-picion of Jewish features. I vowed then never to return to Berchtesgaden again and I wish I had kept that vow.

As it was, I returned 15 years later to find the place changed again, if anything for the worse. The Autobahn to Salzburg had been opened by then, placing Berchtesgaden within a 90-minute car drive of Munich, and the town was besieged by wealthy German businessmen with their families, occupying all the best hotels, elbowing you off the pavements and crowd-ing you out of the cafés. True, the jackbooted Nazi military had long since gone, but their place had been taken by members of the American Army of Occupation, who were there in even greater quantity and – dare I say it? – nothing like so well behaved. Coming on furlough from Munich and other places elsewhere, they kept arriving in a continuous stream, mostly in enormous automobiles that seemed to be constructed en-tirely in chromium plate, their sole object in life appeared to be to get drunk as quickly as possible. The noise they made was deafening and, wherever they went, they left a trail of ejected chewing-gum behind them. As one old Bavarian gentleman said to me, 'The Romans came here and built on stone. The Ameri-cans are trying to rebuild the town on gum.'

Maybe, by the time you read this, the American Army of Occupation will have gone. But I don't think Berchtesgaden will ever return to anything like its one-time charm. Its hoteliers and shopkeepers have been spoilt by the dollars showered upon them and have developed an avarice that will not be wiped out for many generations, if at all.

Just 'around the corner' from Berchtesgaden is the beautiful Königssee and here you will manage to get a certain amount of peace and tranquillity. When I was a small boy I was told that no one had ever been able to plumb the depths of the Königssee and that, like Coleridge's sacred river Alph, its deeper waters ran away 'through caverns measureless to man'. I have since been informed that there is no truth in either of these assertions, but the lake has nevertheless a distinct air of mystery about it. It is quite small, about five kilometres long and very narrow, but it has a haunting splendour, standing as it does in a deep cleft flanked by high, precipitous mountain walls.

There is a little cluster of hotels at the lake's north end, though no one is allowed to build along its banks. So strictly is this rule enforced that even Hitler himself was not permitted to have a site here. There is, however, one single infringement – the little castle and chapel of St Bartolomä, built by monks in the twelfth century and later becoming successively the summer residence of the Prince-Bishops of Salzburg and a hunting lodge used by the Bavarian monarchs. It is now established as an inn and only the innkeeper, a gamewarden and a fisherman are allowed to live there with their families, whilst an itinerant priest comes across the water to say Mass regularly in the chapel. You can visit St Bartolomä by pleasure boat, electrically propelled so as not to disturb the wild birds unduly; or, if you feel energetic, you can hire a small rowing boat and make your own way there.

Perhaps, before you leave the area, you may feel inclined to visit Hitler's 'eagle's nest' on top of the Kehlstein. It is now the property of the German Alpine Club, who use it as a refuge for climbers, and it may be reached from Obersalzberg by bus or car, which will take you to the entrance of the remarkable lift which the Führer had built regardless of cost. I should mention that the *Adlerhorst* should not be confused with his official summer residence, the *Berghof*. This has been purposely destroyed for reasons which should be obvious. The Germans, and particularly the Bavarians, are not keen to encourage pilgrims.

There are so many interesting places in the Bavarian Tirol that it is difficult to know where to call a halt to our visit to the south-eastern Alps. But there are several other towns which you really ought to take a look at before leaving the district.

For instance, there is Aschau, lying at a height of 650 metres not far south-west of the Chiemsee, with its fine medieval Hohenaschau Castle that can be explored every Wednesday during the summer season. And a little further on you will find Sachrang, which is just beginning to find its feet as a winter sports centre and is to be highly recommended if you want somewhere very cheap and quiet.

Then there is Fischbachau-Birkenstein (what splendid names some of these places have!), which boasts the best-preserved basilica in Oberbayern, dating back to the eleventh century. In the Birkenstein part of the town, you will come across a quaint rococo pilgrimage church, and there is also a magnificently decorated farmhouse, the *Jodlhof*, which has been classed as a protected monument. A few kilometres north lies the little, vivid blue Schliersee and, travelling south, you will soon arrive at Bayrischzell, another favourite spot for winter sports and one of the places where the German army does its training on skis. The chair lifts here work during the summer also and, by taking two of them, you can get to a height of 1,450 metres (over 4,700 feet).

East of the Schliersee is another, much larger lake, the Tegernsee, from which the town on its south bank takes its name. Here there is a very ancient church, founded as a Benedictine monastery in 747, which contains some fine ceiling frescoes by Hans Asam (1648) and also the graves of a number of Bavarian poets. On the west bank of the lake is the health resort of Bad Wiessee which, according to the local guidebook, has 'two mineral springs for internal and external use and inhalations'. I am not too sure about the 'inhalation' bit but, if you happen to have a liking for rotten eggs and stewed Brussels sprouts, you should have a whale of a time here!

Bad Tölz, not very far away, has similar delights to offer, but I should not be too scathing of its virtues. If you happen to be a sufferer from high blood pressure or heart troubles, you may well find a palliative, if not a cure, in its clinics. Certainly the Roman settlers did. They called it Tollusium and quite a few Roman scribes have written of the efficacy of its waters. Some Roman remains are still to be seen here and the market street is a particular attraction. There is a Crucifixion Church, built in 1720-6 complete with a replica of the holy Crucifixion stairs in Rome and the 1718 church of St Leonard, dedicated to the patron saint of working horses. Every year, in November, the traditional St Leonard's ride takes place in Bad Tölz, in honour of the saint. And, for some reason or other, the town's 13,000 inhabitants make a habit of wearing the costumes of their fore-bears, which adds a touch of gaiety to what I consider to be one of Bavaria's better spas.

And now, moving southwards along a road that closely follows the course of the river Isar, we pass through the winter resorts of Lenggrins and Krün and come to the most famous Bavarian ski centre of them all, Garmisch-Partenkirchen. It is also the largest, with a population rapidly approaching 30,000, and it can offer accommodation for 11,000 visitors, nearly three times the number that can be boarded in Nürnberg, though only half the capacity of Berchtesgaden.

It was originally two towns, facing each other across the river, but they were amalgamated in 1935, soon after it was heard that the winter Olympics of 1936 were to be staged there. The face of Garmisch was then changed almost beyond recognition by the building of a gigantic stadium, which can hold 100,000 people, 30,000 of them seated, for ski events alone, and two large ice rinks with elaborate floodlighting. More than 20 new hotels were also constructed in the course of a single year.

I always feel that the two names are so descriptive of the place. Garmisch has a garish, metallic sound, and that is exactly how the town appears to the eye. Partenkirchen, on the other hand, is soft and musical and you will find that the old town fits these adjectives perfectly. Even so, the oldest church, built in 1280, happens to be in Garmisch.

Like Berchtesgaden, the place was full of Americans when I last visited it in the winter. But they were less noisy and obtrusive. Perhaps the fact that so many of them were indifferent skiers had done something to their morale. Nevertheless, they had the usual effect upon shop and hotel prices and, if you are looking for a cheap, peaceful winter sports holiday, Garmisch is the one place in Bavaria that I would not recommend.

From Garmisch-Partenkirchen a rack railway will take you to the summit of Bavaria's highest mountain, the Zugspitze, which is 3,010 metres (9,782 feet) above sea level. The journey takes 65 minutes and the train – if such it may be called – climbs slowly and steeply through the pine forests passing the little Eibsee, with its amazingly dark blue water, and then disappearing into a long tunnel to re-emerge at the Schneefernhaus with its magnificent ski-ing grounds. The summit station is actually some 300 metres below the highest point and you will have to climb the rest if you want to enjoy the finest views. If you are feeling energetic, I suggest you take the single journey to the top and then walk back to Garmisch. It will take you the best part of three hours, but it is fairly easy going all the way.

Not far from Garmisch and almost on the Austrian border is the charming little town of Mittenwald, where the houses are gay with eighteenth-century frescoes. For someone who loves rugged Alpine scenery, this is probably the best place of all in which to stay and there is plenty of good accommodation to be had at a reasonable price. I would particularly advise the Post Hotel, where the food is wonderful.

In the seventeenth century, the famous violin-maker, Matthias Klotz, settled in Mittenwald and the town has been renowned for its violins ever since. It even possesses a school for teaching the craft and there is a small museum close to the Post Hotel which displays a fine collection of the instruments, some of which are over 300 years old.

As one might well expect, the road from Garmisch-Partenkirchen to Munich is one of the best and certainly one of the busiest in Oberbayern. A few kilometres to the north of Garmisch it passes through Ettal, where the Benedictine monks spend a lot of time making Bavaria's finest liqueur (the *Ettaler Klosterlikör*), and from here you may make a short diversion to Oberammergau.

So much has been written and said about Oberammergau that it seems rather pointless to describe it in any detail here. It is, of course, world-renowned for its Passion Play, which occurs every time the last digit of the year is a nought and which has been staged ever since the beginning of the seventeenth century as a thanksgiving for the town being liberated from the Black Death. But there are other aspects of Oberammergau which are not so well-known. The natives may well make a lot of money from the Passion Play, but their most stable source of income is woodcarving, an art they carry out to perfection. And I feel sure you will be intrigued by the lovely frescoes – known here as *Lüftmalerei* (literally 'air paintings') – with which many of the houses are decorated. Some of them are extremely elaborate and date back to the early eighteenth century.

I first came to Oberammergau with my parents in 1930 and the roads leading from the Allgäu were so atrocious in those days that we broke a front spring on our car. It was repaired in a few hours by 'St Peter' – who then owned the only decent garage in the town – and he made such a good job of it that the manufacturers afterwards confessed it was the best bit of workmanship in the whole vehicle!

As the main road approaches Munich, it runs within easy distance of the country's two other large lakes, the Ammersee and the Starnbergsee. In recent times these have become extremely popular picnic and weekend spots for the citizens of Munich and, in consequence, they have been somewhat cluttered up with 'lidos', 'marinas' and many other such horrors of this modern age. But they are both steeped in history and should not be missed.

The Ammersee is the smaller of the two, being 16 kilometres long and about eight kilometres across at its widest part. The small towns skirting it are great favourites with yachtsmen and artists and the largest of them, Diessen, was a prosperous fish-market as far back as the thirteenth century. It has a fine monastery church with adjoining monastery buildings that was rebuilt in baroque style by Johann Michael Fischer in 1732-8.

Towering above the lake is the Heiliger Berg (Holy Mountain) with the village of Andechs, a place of pilgrimage and the site of a Benedictine priory. The walk up to Andechs through the woods, a gradual and easy climb, is one of the best I have ever enjoyed and will provide you with some splendid views. I am told that if you should take it on a Good Friday you will see the monks processing to Andechs, carrying a huge wooden cross and re-enacting the Saviour's last long climb to Calvary.

The Starnbergsee, which is 20 kilometres long but not quite so wide as the Ammersee, has a regular steamboat service during the summer season, which puts in at all the places of interest. The town of Starnberg, with its sixteenth-century castle of the Prince-Bishops, rises on terraces at the north end of the lake and was actually built on the site of an old but presumably un-successful vineyard. From it you may visit the Herrgottsruh (God's Rest) Chapel, which has some prehistoric tombstones dating back to pagan times, and climb to the top of the Hinden-burghöhe.

Tutzing, halfway along the east bank, has been developed as a highly fashionable summer resort for wealthy Bavarian busi-nessmen, whose villas strive to outdo each other in vulgarity, but it is probably the best place on the lake from which to bathe. However, I think you might prefer Seeshaupt, at the extreme south end. It is delightfully quiet during most of the summer and, when you get tired of looking at the lake, you can turn around and feast your eyes on the Alpine background.

Finally, don't forget to visit Schloss Berg whilst you are on the Starnbergsee. It is not a particularly attractive castle to look at, but it has some very poignant associations. For it was here that the unhappy Ludwig II spent the last days of his unfortunate life. Still pathetically young, he was virtually incarcerated in Schloss Berg and accompanied everywhere he went by a medical attendant, to whom he was shackled whenever he was allowed to venture outside. He met his end by plunging into the waters of the lake, taking his attendant with him.

9. Munich

'I've lived in this great old city for nearly six years. I know its streets as well as I know the veins on the backs of my own hands. But I still haven't seen more than a quarter of what there is to see.' Those words, spoken to me by an American army officer at the airport only a few years ago, just about sum up Munich. There is so much to see, so much to admire, that it would take the best part of a lifetime to cover everything.

There is only one word in the American's statement with which I would disagree. Munich, as it stands today, is not 'old'. Compared with many of the other Bavarian towns we have discussed up to now, it is a mere stripling. True it was first founded by Henry the Lion, duke of Saxony and Bavaria, in the twelfth century and remained during the Middle Ages one of the most important political centres in the country. But, like the Franconian town of Mergentheim, it died a lingering death in the eighteenth century, only to rise again like a resplendent phoenix in the nineteenth century when, like Berlin, it was raised from comparative obscurity to become a capital city. Then, once again it died – this time an angry and violent death under the onslaught of Allied bombers – and only in recent years has it regained its former grandeur.

The ground upon which Munich stands is probably the most unfertile in the whole of Bavaria. If you were to dig only a short distance down, you would find layer upon layer of rock debris, brought down from the mountains during the Ice Age. It is, in fact, the same sort of moraine that you can see today at the foot of any large glacier.

Because the area was so barren, the Romans spurned it. But there was an early monastic settlement on the site where Henry the Lion built his original city which was known as *zu den Mönchen*, which can be freely translated as 'at the monks' place'. The name later became corrupted and abbreviated to *München*, which remains today as the correct German word for Munich. A monk is still prominently featured in the city's coat of arms.

King Ludwig I was largely responsible for restoring Munich in the nineteenth century and for filling its palaces, churches, art galleries and museums with so many priceless treasures. During the 23 years of his reign, the sums of money spent in this manner attained astronomical proportions, yet the State Treasury did not appear to be unduly embarrassed by them. And, of course, rare works of art could be acquired in those days for minute fractions of the prices they would fetch in today's auction rooms. The Leonardo da Vinci in the Alte Pinakothek gallery, for example, would fetch well over a million pounds if it was sold now, yet it changed hands less than two centuries ago for the equivalent of 300.

You must remember, however, that the Munich you will see today is not exactly as Ludwig built it. As I have already said, the bomb damage during the war was truly horrific, with the result that the old city lost nearly three-quarters of its buildings. Nevertheless, a large proportion of its art treasures remained unharmed – having been prudently stored away in safe places – and, as with Würzburg, most of the more important structures have now been rebuilt to the original designs. The old architects' plans were brought out of the archives and followed as faithfully as possible.

I think the most logical place to begin a sightseeing tour is the main railway station which, in the case of Munich, happens to be almost in the city centre. Taking one of the streets facing you on the opposite side of the Bahnhofplatz will lead you into the Karlsplatz, with the magnificent Palais de Justice on your left. Crossing this, you will enter a wide and busy thoroughfare, the Neuhauserstrasse, at the bottom of which stands the massive cathedral (Frauenkirche), with its twin cupola-capped towers, each 100 metres (320 feet) high. One of the largest Gothic churches in Europe, it was built between 1468 and 1488 by Jörg Ganghofer and contains the tomb of Ludwig the Bavarian by Hans Krumper and a vault in which lie buried many early princes and bishops, both of which structures mercifully survived the bombing.

Neuhauserstrasse has by now become Kaufingerstrasse and, at the bottom of this, is the Marienplatz with the fine New Town Hall. This was built in two stages – 1867-74 and 1888-1908 – by Georg Hauberisser and its rich neo-Gothic façade, reminiscent of the English Houses of Parliament, fortunately escaped serious damage during the war, what there was being made good when the Town Hall was rebuilt in 1952-6. The tall central tower has two arched windows, one above the other, set not far above the ground, in which life-size figures begin to move as soon as the clock strikes 11 in the morning. A tournament is 'performed' in the upper window, whilst coopers execute a stately dance in the lower window.

The opposite side of the Marienplatz leads into the Tal, Munich's oldest street, and here you will see the remains of the Old Town Hall, built by Jörg Ganghofer at the same time as he was building the cathedral. Not far away, just to the south of the square, is Munich's oldest church (Peterskirche), founded in 1278-94 and rebuilt a number of times since. Its tower, nearly as high as those of the Frauenkirche, is affectionately known to the Müncheners as *Der Alte Peter* (Old Peter) and, if you feel so inclined, you can climb up to its observation platform just below the cupola. But one word of advice before you do. Step back from the church and take a good look at the platform. If you see a white disc displayed up there, it means that visibility is good. If the disc is red, the view from the top will be poor and it will be hardly worth your while making the effort. Inside the church, you will find works by Erasmus Grasser, Ignatius Günther, Johannes Baptiste Zimmermann and Egidus Quirinus Asam.

You are now close to the old Viktualienmarkt, where you will find the cheery 'girl' flowersellers with their gaily bedecked stalls. Alongside is the aptly named Blumenstrasse and halfway down this is St Jakobsplatz with the Münchner Stadtmuseum, containing a permanent exhibition showing life and culture in Munich from the seventeenth to the twentieth centuries. I strongly advise you to take a good look at this before continuing with your tour as it will help you to understand much of what you see later on.

Striking north-westwards out of St Jakobsplatz will lead you across the Oberanger into Sendlingerstrasse, where stands the Johann von Nepomunk church. It was built in 1733-46 and is probably the most outstanding example of the Asam Brothers' work, with its richly decorated interior. An interesting fact about this church is that the Asams personally financed the whole project, raising it on a site next door to their own home just for the sheer joy of creating something beautiful.

Carrying on down the Sendlingerstrasse will bring you to the fourteenth-century Sendlingertor, another of the few really old structures left in the city. Opposite it, on the other side of the Sendlingerplatz, is a large, rather garish church, St Matthew's, built in 1952 by Alwin Gsaenger. If you now take the wide Sonnenstrasse leading northwards out of the Sendlingerplatz, it will bring you back to the Karlsplatz and you will have completed a full circle. Off the Sonnenstrasse, incidentally, is the Schwanthalerstrasse in which stands the Deutsches Theater, where modern plays and musicals are performed.

Munich is said to have more museums than any other city in the world and I can well believe it. Almost any street of any size at all contains at least one museum, though some of them are so small that you may easily pass them by. However, the largest of them all, the Deutsches Museum, lies not in a street but on its own island, situated between the Ludwigsbrücke and the Corneliusbrücke in the middle of the river Isar. Its full and correct name is the German Museum of Masterworks of Natural Science and Technology, which looks even more awe-inspiring in German than it does in English but does at least explain its purpose. It is, in fact, the largest museum of its kind in the world and contains, besides many fascinating full-scale working models, a superb planetarium. It would take you at least a week to go through its many rooms and halls with any thoroughness so, if your stay in Munich is to be a short one and you are not all that interested in science, you might well find it advisable to give it a miss. Indeed, it may be necessary to visit only that museum or those museums dealing with subjects that particularly appeal to you, in which case I feel I should depart from my usual practice and list them categorically.

As I have stated, the Deutsches Museum is near the Corneliusbrücke and may be reached by taking a 52 tram from the Peterskirche. The Bayerische Nationalmuseum (in the Prinzregentenstrasse, trams 53 and 55) deals mainly with Bavarian arts and crafts through the ages and contains an unique collection of Christmas cribs and articles from the old Bavarian Army Museum. The Museum für Völkerkunde (near the Maximilian II memorial, buses 1 and 21) has some fine examples of Indian and Peruvian art. The Residenzmuseum (in the Residenz, behind the Nationaltheater in the Maximilianstrasse) displays a fine collection of classical busts, also suites of rooms showing furnishings from the sixteenth to nineteenth centuries. The Schatzkammer or Treasury (again in the Residenz) is a place in which to see magnificent examples of goldsmiths' and jewellers' craft in the Middle Ages, baroque and Renaissance periods. The Deutsches Jagdmuseum (near the Frauenkirche) is mainly concerned with animals of the chase and with old hunting gear. Die Neue Sammlung (which is part of the Bayerisches Nationalmuseum) deals with applied art. The Museum Antiker Kleinkunst (in the Prinz-Karl-Palais, Königinstrasse, north of the Residenz and on the north side of the Hofgarten) houses constantly changing collections of small antiques. The State Graphic Collection (in the Meiserstrasse, tram 55) contains drawings and prints from the late Gothic period. And, of course, the Theatermuseum (close by the Prinz-Karl-Palais in Galeriestrasse), is self-explanatory.

I have mentioned only those museums which are of particular interest. A full list of all there is to be seen can be obtained from Munich's main information bureau in the Rosental, near the Peterskirche.

The art galleries in Munich are not so numerous, but you will probably find them more fascinating. And here again you may be compelled by pressure of time to make a choice, although you are going to find this a difficult task. The one you must on no account miss is the Alte Pinakothek (in the Barerstrasse, a short distance from the centre of the town, buses 5 and 8) which was rebuilt and reopened in 1957. As its name suggests, it was designed to house only the works of the Old Masters, whereas the Neue Pinakothek, not yet restored at the time of writing, was intended for more modern paintings. The origin of the Alte Pinakothek stemmed from a small art collection begun by Duke Wilhelm IV in the sixteenth century and some of the paintings he purchased are on view.

Not much more than 1,000 of the 7,000 priceless masterpieces owned by the gallery are actually on show at any one time, although they are changed around from time to time. Permanent exhibits include Dürer's *Self Portrait in Fur Coat*, Titian's *Emperor Charles V* (painted when the artist was living in Augsburg), Raphael's *Holy Family from House Canigiani* and da Vinci's *Madonna with Child*, besides many works by Holbein, Memling, Altdorfer, Rubens, Rembrandt, Van Dyck, Breughel, Franz Hals, Velasquez, El Greco, Murillo, Goya, Botticelli, Tintoretto and others equally famous. I would hate to set a value on the whole collection, but I have been told that it is well in excess of 250 million pounds.

For examples of nineteenth- and twentieth-century art, you must go to the *Haus der Kunst*, located on the west side of the National Museum in Prinzregentenstrasse, which displays works mainly of German and French impressionists, once housed in the Neue Pinakothek and the Neue Staatsgalerie. German painters of the late nineteenth century are represented in the Schackgalerie, to the east of the museum, and both galleries may be reached quickly by 53 or 55 tram, the latter starting from the town centre.

I have made a special point of mentioning Munich's trams and buses, because I consider them to be one of the best transport systems in Europe. Their conductors are most courteous and helpful – nearly all of them have a smattering of English, speaking with a strong American accent! – and the various services run frequently and on time, though you should avoid the rush hours between 7 and 9 in the morning and 5 and 7 in the evening. You can see a great deal of Munich on foot, but it is absolutely senseless using a car when you have a comfortable bus or tram virtually at your elbow.

Works of the Munich painters will be found in the Städtischegalerie in the Luisenstrasse just off the Königsplatz, for which you take a 2 or a 7 bus from the main railway station. Among those represented are Franz von Lenbach, in whose old house the gallery is situated, and Paul Klee, a son of Munich who became a naturalised Swiss shortly before he died. In the Königsplatz itself are the Glyptothek and the Staatliche Antikensammlungen, both of which contain many items of interest for the lover of classical figures and vases, whilst the square is dominated by the Propyläaen, a massive gate in imitation of the propylaea of the Acropolis which, I am ashamed to say, always gives me the shudders. Like some of the other buildings in Munich, it is almost too monstrous to be true!

North-east of the city, close to the Nationalmuseum and above

20   *Oberammergau: a street*

the Haus der Kunst, is the so-called Englischer Garten. This was
the brainchild of a very remarkable character, a man with virtually three different nationalities. Born in Massachusetts in 1753
the son of English immigrant parents, Ben Thompson fought
with the British against the Americans in 1775 and was eventually brought back to England and rewarded with a knighthood
for his services. He thereafter became a diplomat and, in the
course of his missions abroad, met the Elector of Bavaria. To
him he suggested the idea of a great pleasure park in the growing new city of Munich and, when Ludwig I came to the throne,
this ambition was fulfilled. Thompson was made a Count of the
Holy Roman Empire by the Elector, taking the English title of
Rumford, and you will find a house and a monument to his
memory in the Englischer Garten. He is also commemorated by
a statue which stands near the Maximilian II memorial.

The Englischer Garten is a sort of cross between London's
Hyde Park and Kew Gardens. It contains all the usual public
park trappings, including a boating lake, a Chinese 'willow pat-
tern' bridge, a pagoda and another pseudo-Grecian piece of
architecture called the Monopteros. If you wish, you can take
a ride through the park in an open carriage or take a meal in
the open-air Aumeister restaurant.

The rulers of Bavaria lived in the Residenz, to which I have
already referred briefly. It is not a particularly beautiful building, being composed of a number of different structures brought
together as one. And, although I have seen it described in one
guidebook as 'an unique representative of Renaissance, baroque,
rococo and neo-Classical styles', most people regard it as something of a hotch-potch. It, too, was badly damaged by bombs
and I don't think rebuilding has brought much improvement. It
was originally begun about 1400, but it fell into decay during
the early eighteenth century, to be restored and enlarged by
Ludwig I, who instructed the architect Leo von Klenze to add
the Königsbau (King's Building) and Festsaalbau (Banqueting
Hall). Besides containing a museum, the Residenz also houses the

21 *Landsberg: the main square with the Schmalzturm*

Cuvilliés Theater, a magnificent rococo structure sparkling with chandeliers, which was rebuilt after the war at a cost of nearly half a million pounds and ceremoniously reopened on the occasion of Munich's eight-hundredth anniversary in 1958.

I never look at the Residenz without thinking of Lola Montez, who occupied a suite of its rooms during the hectic years in which she was mistress of Ludwig I. What a woman! Born in Limerick in 1818 and christened Marie Dolores Eliza Rosanna Gilbert, she came to England in her early teens as a servant girl, married her employer's son – a young ensign in the army – and, after a series of scandals at home and in India, was hustled off as a divorcee to Spain – the native country of her maternal ancestors – where she learnt to be a dancer. By the time she was 26, she had reappeared in London as a 'Spanish' ballerina, seduced Franz Liszt in Paris, slept with the King of Württemburg and was now ensconced in the Residenz, drawing upon Ludwig's treasury for vast sums of money and honoured by him with the title of countess! No wonder Horace Wyndham entitled his excellent biography of her *The Magnificent Montez*!

Close to the Residenz is the Feldherrnhalle (Hall of the Generals), an open building containing the statues of famous Bavarian military leaders. Ludwig I seems to have had a craze for imitation and this is a replica of the Loggia dei Lanzi in Florence. Just beyond it is the baroque Theatinerkirche, spiritual home of the Theatin monks, founded in 1663, reconstructed in 1768 and the work of a number of designers, including Agostino Barelli, Enrico Zuccali and Francois Cuvilliés. It was later remodelled to its present form at Ludwig's instructions.

If you return now to the Maximilianstrasse and walk eastwards, you will pass the imposing new Nationaltheater on your left and come to the Maximilian II monument. Carrying straight on, you will cross the Maximiliansbrücke, which also spans a small island in the river, and arrive at the Maximilianeum, a very large and rather austere building which has been the seat of the Bavarian Government since 1877. It stands in an imposing circular *Platz* and is surrounded by an attractive park. If you now follow the eastern boundary of this southwards, you will pass the public swimming baths and arrive at the Ludwigs-brücke. Crossing this brings you back to the old town with the fourteenth-century Isar gate in the Isartorplatz and so into the Tal. In a street off to the right of this stands the famous Hof-bräuhaus, an eternal reminder of the fact that Munich is one of the most famous brewing centres in the world.

Ask any Münchner to name the four seasons of the year and he will give you the answer in terms of beer. In March they celebrate their strong brews and in May they go wild about *Maibock*, the strongest of them all. The lighter *lager* beers are all the rage in July and August and then comes the great *Oktober-fest*, when the whole town gives itself up to merry-making, with carnivals, dancing and costume processions. If you have an urge to try the various brews, I suggest you spend an evening in the Hofbräuhaus, where you can drink them from mugs of all shapes and sizes, at the same time listening to a typically Bavarian brass band. Or you could go to the *Matthäser Bierstadt* in the Bayerstrasse, claimed to be the largest beer hall in the world.

Food is another of Munich's great attractions and I can particularly recommend their *Brathendle*, chicken cooked on a spit; their *Kalbsvögerl*, stuffed veal cutlets; and their *Steckerlfisch*, river fish delicately seasoned and grilled on sticks. Many dishes are served with special Bavarian noodles – dumplings made from bread or potatoes – which may sound uninviting but are delicious to eat. Providing you do not have to watch expenses too carefully, you should try dining at the *Schwärzwalder*, in the Hartmannstrasse, where they also have the biggest wine list I have ever seen in my life. Or, as an alternative, go to *Humpl-mayr*, in the Maximilianplatz, one of the most famous restaurants in the world. For a less expensive meal, you will find no place to beat the *Ratskeller*, beneath the Town Hall. And, if it's a fine day and you fancy a short but really enjoyable trip out of town, take the 52 tram from Peterskirche to the end of its

13-kilometre journey and dine amidst beautiful rural surroundings at the *Grünwalder Weinbauer*. There is an interesting thirteenth-century hunting castle nearby.

There are, in fact, several excursions out of Munich which ought to be taken. First and foremost is the one to Schloss Nymphenburg, about 10 kilometres from the city centre. This is best reached by a 21 bus from the main railway station, which passes the Botanical Gardens en route.

Schloss Nymphenburg, usually known as the Nymphenburg Palace, was started in 1664 and took more than 100 years to build. It was formerly used by the rulers of Bavaria as a summer residence and its fantastic grounds contain four subsidiary castles, each constructed according to the whims of the ruler at the period. The most interesting of these are the Amalienburg, built between 1734 and 1739 by Francois Cuvilliés the Elder, and the Pagodenburg (Castle of the Pagodas), the work of Josef Effner in 1716-19. Inside the Palace itself is a magnificent rococo Festsaal, where concerts are held during the summer season, and the Marstall Museum, housing a fine collection of carriages and coaches. You should also visit Ludwig I's *Schönheitengalerie* (Gallery of Beauties), with its pictures of lovely women including Lola Montez herself.

Across the road from the Palace are the workshops of the renowned Nymphenburg porcelain factory, founded in the eighteenth century by the Wittelsbachs. It is open to visitors and you may purchase its products on the spot.

Nineteen kilometres to the north of Munich lies the small town of Schlessheim, a 20-minute journey from the main railway station. Here are three castles well worth a visit, even though they were all badly damaged during the war. The Altes Schloss, built as a summer residence for the dukes of Bavaria in 1597 and reconstructed in 1616, was worst hit of all, but rebuilding was well in hand the last time I saw it. The Neues Schloss, designed by Enrico Zuccali and Josef Effner in 1700-21, has been completely restored to its former beauty as has also the Gartenschloss Lustheim, another of Zuccali's works dating back to 1689.

I cannot understand how these places came to be subjected to air attack. I visited Schlessheim in 1938 and there was certainly nothing of any strategic importance there then, nor were any important factories built during the war. True a fairly busy railway line passes through Schlessheim, but there are plenty of places where it could have been bombed without causing damage to historic buildings. And I have also been told that Schlessheim was a garrison town for a short time, but there were no troops stationed there during the great bombardments of 1944 and 1945.

Could it possibly have been on account of Dachau? This notorious concentration camp lay only a few kilometres to the east of Schlessheim and the raids may have been staged to boost the morale of the poor wretches confined within its perimeter. Today only a simple, tastefully designed monument marks the site of the grim camp and the people of Dachau – once one of the prettiest little towns to be found on the outskirts of Munich – have almost forgotten the evil that was once in their midst. They have revived their local festivals, including the traditional oxen race in August, but the old gaiety is no longer there. And I feel at least two more generations must come and go before no one is left to remember.

The main road from Schlessheim to Munich passes by the television tower on the Oberwiesenfeld, which is nearly 300 metres high. There is an observation platform at 2000 metres reached by express lift, from which you may obtain a magnificent aerial view of the whole city and its environs. In Munich itself, you can obtain a similar, closer view from the tower of the New Town Hall, 90 metres up and also served by a lift. Or, as I have already explained, you can always climb to the top of *Der Alte Peter*.

You can also get another bird's-eye glimpse from the head of the statue of Bavaria in the Theresienwiese Park, a short distance south of the Hauptbahnhof. You will have to climb 130 steps and you will be well advised not to attempt this on a hot day, since the statue is made of bronze and the temperature inside can reach to well above 40 degrees C! I made the effort myself one August afternoon not very long ago and I'm quite sure I lost two kilograms in weight!

It is in the Theresienwiese that the major activities of the Oktoberfest are staged, with bands playing and displays of folk dancing. To the immediate west of it lies the Ausstellungpark (Amusement Park) which, before the war, used to be one of the best of its kind in Europe. Today many of its old, unique attractions have gone, to be replaced by a raucous rather enforced atmosphere of gaiety. However, if you enjoy good boxing or are what a certain English T.V. commentator describes as a 'grappling fan', you will be able to see some interesting bouts here.

Along the south side of the main railway station is the Landsbergerstrasse, the beginning of the main road leading to the Allgäu. After some 40 kilometres (25 miles), this road passes the north end of the Ammersee and then takes you straight on to the town of Landsberg, on the river Lech, which is where you enter the Allgäu proper.

Landsberg is probably one of the finest medieval cities in southern Bavaria and is in a fairly good state of preservation, although little remains of its ancient fortifications except a number of thirteenth- to fifteenth-century towers, including the Bayertor, the Sandauertor, the Schmaltzturm, the Nonnenturm (Nun's Tower) and the superb Färbertor, which has been the city's main gate since 1425. The fortress of Landsberg was where Adolf Hitler was imprisoned for a short period.

The main buildings of interest are, however, mostly eighteenth-century and are nearly all the work of Dominikus Zimmerman. Indeed, I have heard Landsberg described on more than one occasion as a permanent Zimmerman exhibition! His masterpieces include the church of St John (1741-54), the Monastery Church (1720-5), the Maltese Church (1752-4) and the façade of the beautiful Rathaus (1720). The oldest ecclesiastical building in the town is the fourteenth-century Parish Church of the Assumption, converted to baroque in the seventeenth century. It contains a fine figure of the Virgin, the Madonna of Multscher.

Every five years, Landsberg stages its celebrated Rühtenfest, when all the town's children parade in historical costumes.

From Landsberg it is about 30 kilometres (19 miles) to Kaufbeuren and it is from here that you will see the full glory of the Allgäu stretched out in front of you. Part of the original town, dating from the early thirteenth century, still remains and includes the quaint Fünfknopf (Five Button) Tower. The late Gothic Chapel of St Blaise contains a magnificently carved altar by Jörg Lederer. Kaufbeuren also puts on the oldest of all Bavaria's many children's dance festivals every July, which was originally instituted at the behest of Maximilian I.

A short distance to the north of the town is Irsee, with its pretty little lake, not much more than a large pond, and its old Monastery Church, rebuilt by Franz Beer in 1699 and containing some very fine stuccoes by Josef Schmuzer. A few kilometres further on is Mindelheim, of particular interest to English visitors since Winston Churchill's noble ancestor, the first Duke of Marlborough, was created Prince of Mindelheim by the Emperor Leopold in 1704 and the title is still one borne by the present Duke.

The first stretch of the Romantic Road runs between Kaufbeuren and Füssen, meeting up with the river Lech at Rosshaupten and then slowly rising through a green, wooded valley with the mountains beginning to close in on three sides. It is a fitting approach to some of the loveliest scenery in the whole of Bavaria.

10. The Allgäu

I have left the Allgäu almost to the last, for reasons which I hope the reader will appreciate and forgive. Next to Liechenstein, which I have come to regard as a second home, it is the part of Europe that I know and love best. My father came here as early as 1898 and I followed in his footsteps 25 years later, spending much of my boyhood in and around Füssen. And when I took my children abroad for the first time in 1961, our itinerary had to include the Allgäu. It is a perfect spot for youngsters, with its lakes and mountains, its castles and its legends.

Füssen, a town of some 11,000 inhabitants that lies at the southernmost end of the Romantic Road, is usually referred to as the 'capital of the Allgäu', although I have never been able to discover whether this description is backed by any deed or charter. It is also normally associated with its satellite town Bad Faulenbach, which was the first spa noted by the Romans when they came to Bavaria. Here they continue to do a brisk trade in curative waters, mud baths and Kneipp therapy and they operate a special sanatorium for internal disorders. In other words, if you have crippled yourself and rotted your insides with too much eating and drinking, Bad Faulenbach is a good place in which to stay. And I don't say this with tongue in cheek. I have seen some remarkable cures effected there in a very short space of time.

The old town of Füssen was originally no more than a large fort, built by the Romans to guard a pass through the Alps. This pass still exists as a main road, which crosses the Austrian border at Reutte, climbs through the Lechtal to Lech, then descends to Stuben, whence it links with the Arlberg Pass. Very little of the old fort now remains, the site being occupied by the Hohe Schloss (High Castle), which was raised in the 11th century, extended in 1322 and once occupied by the Prince-Bishops of Augsburg during the summer months. You should take a look at its Hall of Princes, which has a remarkable wooden ceiling designed by Jörg Lederer in 1500.

Entering Füssen from the west is quite an experience. The road from Lake Constance wanders up and down through rather dull, agricultural territory for kilometre after kilometre and then – suddenly – you turn a corner and the whole glory of the Allgäu lies spread out in front of you. You see Füssen, with its rather grim, red-roofed castle dominating it from the top of a low hill. You see the Forggensee, surrounded by smaller lakes, some of them no larger than big ponds. And, behind it all, you see a great range of mountains, many of them with snow-capped peaks even in the height of summer. You feel at once that you are entering a wonderland and you will not be proved wrong.

It is worth while spending a whole day in Füssen, even if you do not intend to stay there, because there is so much to see and enjoy. Take a look at the St Mang monastery, founded by the Benedictines in the ninth century, and its splendid crypt, which has one of the oldest frescoes in Bavaria. Both the monastery and its church were subsequently rebuilt in baroque style by Johann Jakob Herkomer at the beginning of the 18th century. Then inspect the nearby St Anne's Chapel, with its famous painting of the *Totentanz* (Dance of Death) by Jakob Hiebeler (1602). Go on from there to see the *Gottesacker* church of St Sebastion, named 'God's Acre' because it was the town's principal graveyard in medieval times. And, when you visit the Hohe Schloss, make a point of looking at its picture gallery, which contains paintings by some of the earliest Swabian masters.

If you don't happen to be historically-minded, just find yourself a stout walking-stick and go tramping in the woods around Füssen, leaving that confounded car behind for once in one of the town's many free parking places. You will be surprised how fit you will feel after only a short stroll and your efforts will be rewarded by some magnificent views.

This part of the Allgäu has been well described as 'The Swan Country'. Every lake, large or small, has its family of swans and, on the east bank of the Forggensee, you will actually find a small town that has been named after them, Schwangau. Travelling south out of here – or, alternatively, taking the main road from Füssen – will bring you to the Schwansee (Swan Lake) and, a little further on, to the Alpsee and the Castles of Hohenschwangau and Neuschwanstein.

The origins of Hohenschwangau castle go back to the fourteenth century, but the present building, which is not particularly striking, was reconstructed in 1833-7 at the order of King Maximilian II and to plans by Quaglio. It became later a thorn in the side of Ludwig II, who thoroughly detested its drab insignificance and thereupon commanded another castle to be built for his personal use on a slightly higher hill across the valley.

Hence Neuschwanstein, begun in 1869 and completed in 1886, at a cost of what would then be the equivalent of well over a million pounds. Regarded by many people as a 'folly', it is none the less a magnificent example of architectural extravagance and I am ashamed to confess that I personally consider it to be one of the loveliest sights in the world. Those who remember the 'ivory castle' used in Gibbs' Dentifrice advertiseing in between the wars will find its replica here, complete with towers, turrets and pinnacles that thrust themselves madly towards the skies.

Neuschwanstein must be the only castle in the world that was directly inspired by a musician. As soon as you enter it, you begin to feel the influence of Richard Wagner, Ludwig's protégé. There are paintings telling the story of *Tannhäuser* in the king's private apartments and the great Singers' Hall is festooned with scenes from *Parsifal*. Poor, mad Ludwig wanted the place to be regarded as the Castle of the Holy Grail and even avowed that the Holy Grail – the platter used by Christ at the Last Supper – was kept in the castle's throne room.

Ludwig was also fascinated by swans. As a small boy, he had gazed many times with awe at the amazing *Schwanenrittersaal* (Swan Knight's Hall) in the Castle of Hohenschwangau and he had become obsessed with the idea that he was the hereditary 'King of the Swans'. There was, perhaps, not so much madness in this as appears at first sight. Swans in Bavaria, as in England, were considered to be the prerogative of the monarch and were protected by royal charter. We should, indeed, be grateful to Ludwig II, not only for the music of Wagner, not only for giving us so much to delight the eye, but also for respecting and preserving the ancestors of those delightful birds that still continue to grace the lakes of beautiful Allgäu. Insane though he was alleged to have been, he yet possessed a gentleness and sense of artistry that are seldom to be found in kings.

I have never yet met a visitor to Neuschwanstein who has not wanted to photograph it. Unfortunately, it is by no means easy to obtain a good picture, owing to the position in which the castle is situated, and it usually entails quite a climb before you can find a suitable angle. However, I can suggest a happy compromise. If you take the path immediately facing the main entrance and walk up it for about ten minutes, you will be able to get quite a satisfactory shot through the trees. It is best to do this in the morning, when the sun is in the south-east and not too high in the sky, particularly if you are using colour film.

There is another path nearby, which leads down to a gorge through which flows the Pöllat, a tributary of the river Lech. It is by no means a long or difficult walk and it will reward you with fascinating views of the stream cascading and boiling its way between deep clefts in the rock until it eventually reaches the valley below. From the end of the path you can either return to Hohenschwangau or carry on to the little town of Schwangau, with its gay little hotels and cafés.

I have scrupulously tried to avoid recommending any hotels by name, on the premise that one man's meat may well be another's poison, but I shall have to break this rule for a second time and mention a little guesthouse of which I am inordinately fond. This is the *Gasthof am See* in the village of Waltenhofen, which is really a part of Schwangau. It is run by a charming fellow called Max Schneidberger and is one of the most comfortable places in which I have ever stayed. It looks right out on to the lake – the motorboat service landing stage is hard by – and one of its specialities is grilled trout, caught only an hour or two before reaching the table.

Ironically enough, the only really bad hotel I have ever come across in Bavaria was in the Allgäu. I won't do its miserable proprietor an injury by naming it, merely contenting myself with stating that it lies on another lake not five kilometres from Füssen. The place looks quite charming from the outside and it was for this reason that I departed from my usual practice and booked rooms by long-distance telephone for my small party without inspecting them first.

The result was catastrophic! The bedrooms were almost devoid of all furniture and the mattresses seemed to have been stuffed with small coke. There was only one bathroom – without hot water – and the loos had doors that would not lock and ceilings that sloped so steeply that it was impossible to stand up. The food was absolutely atrocious – we were offered a choice of either boiled sausage or lukewarm chopped veal in an extremely dubious sauce at both lunch and supper – and the drinks were mediocre. To add to our woes, the *patron* had made a mistake in our bookings and there was no room for an unattached female member of my party. She was invited to share a room with two young bachelors who were accompanying us and there was considerable amazement when she blushingly refused. Only after considerable argument was she allowed to have a staff bed-

room in the attic. Finally, after we had left in something of a
hurry the following day, I discovered that I had lost ten pounds
in English money. That may well have been my own fault, but
I have never been quite sure.

I have mentioned this incident solely for the purpose of em-
phasising that you should always inspect accommodation before
taking it, even in Bavaria. In the Allgäu particularly, there is
never any need to book blindly and in advance. Even if you
can't find room in any of the fashionable resorts, you are sure to
do so in one of the outlying towns and villages and you will
probably fare better. When in doubt, there is one golden rule.
Go to the nearest *Post* Hotel.

From Füssen it is an easy drive of 47 kilometres (30 miles) to
Kempten. This *is* the official capital of the Allgäu, in spite of
what the Füsseners may say to the contrary, and well it should
be, for it is by far the oldest and most historical town in the
province and now has the largest population (50,000). It was
originally a Celtic settlement and was later occupied for three
centuries by the Romans, who called it Cambudonum. Students
of ancient history may be interested to learn that Kempten was
actually mentioned in the writings of Strabo, the Greek geo-
grapher and historian who was one of the greatest travellers of
his day and who lived from 63 B.C. to A.D. 19.

The town lies on the upper reaches of the river Iller and is an
important market for cattle and for dairy produce, being also
a centre for the manufacture of plastics from milk. It was
founded by the monks of St Gall in the eighth century and remains of the old monastery are still to be seen in the beautiful
Kornhausplatz, which was for many centuries the leading corn-
market in south-west Bavaria. The old Kornhaus itself still
stands as a museum, whilst there is another fine collection,
mainly of Roman relics, in the nearby Zumstein House. On the
opposite side of the Kornhausplatz is the church of St Lorenz,
the first baroque church to be built after the Thirty Years' War,
being the work of Michael Beer and Johannes Serro. It contains

a Gothic crucifix dating from about 1380. Next to the church is the Residenz, also by Michael Beer, which was built in 1651-74, becoming the seat of the Lord-Abbots, who ruled here in much the same way as the Prince-Bishops ruled in other towns. The Rathaus, which was originally built in 1474 and then re-designed about 100 years later, has some very interesting late Gothic wooden ceilings.

Twenty-six kilometres (16 miles) south of Kempten is the more modern town of Immenstadt, slowly building a reputation for itself as a winter sports resort. It has not a great deal to offer the lover of architecture, but it possesses some excellent, really low-priced hotels and makes an ideal base for exploring the south-western area of the Allgäu, since it is well supplied with road and rail connections.

You will find this small corner south of Immenstadt quite unique, almost like a separate tiny country cut off from the rest of Bavaria. Indeed, as you will learn presently, some parts of it are not even Bavarian in the true sense of the word.

The road leading south out of Immenstadt closely follows the river Iller and soon begins to climb steadily but very gently up a beautiful valley, passing through a series of large villages with quaint-sounding names like Ofterschwang and Bolsterlang until it arrives at Fischen. This is another of those reasonably-priced winter sports centres about which I have already written and may be recommended for a good, cheap ski-ing holiday. Its sixteenth-century Chapel of Our Lady, containing some unusual votive tablets (pictures offered in fulfilment of a vow), is one of the oldest churches in these parts. Further on, after passing through Obermaiselstein, you will come to the pleasant little Alpine town of Tiefenbach, or you can take the newly con-structed highway direct to Oberstdorf.

I first came to Oberstdorf in 1926, when it was a small village of no more than a few hundred inhabitants and virtually the highest place in the valley that you could reach comfortably by road. Today it is a thriving town with a population of 10,000 and could rightly be described as the 'winter paradise' of the Allgäu, providing you like your paradise a trifle noisy and over-crowded. It is ideally situated, at a height of about 850 metres, on a large, lush plateau, almost completely encircled by two tributaries of the Iller and cupped by mountains, some of which are well over 2,500 metres high. During the winter, you can reach the high slopes of these mountains by means of four chair lifts, two ski lifts and also two cable cars. One of these goes almost to the summit of the Nebelhorn (2,224 metres, 7,228 feet) and continues to operate during the summer season.

Oberstdorf boasts one of the longest ski jumps in the world, on the Schattenberg, which may be reached by the Nebelhorn-bahn, and a fine ice stadium which can be used all the year round. In recent years, it has made almost a fetish of its fash-ionable après-ski entertainments and this, to me, has caused it to lose much of its original charm. It is also beginning to raise its prices steeply, so that they are approaching those charged in Garmisch-Partenkirchen.

However, Oberstdorf is a reasonable place in which to spend a holiday in summer. The seven valleys radiating from the town offer hosts of attractions to the walker and motor traffic is barred from many of the roads leading to the surrounding vil-lages, so that you may roam at will. If golf appeals to you, there is a good little nine-hole course close to the town and for the swimmer there are two spacious outdoor pools. Most of the mountain peaks are easily accessible on foot, so that they pro-vide good training grounds for the climber with more serious ambitions in the future. One of the prettiest walks I know is to the Freibergsee lake, south of Oberstdorf, then up to the Christ-lesee and back by way of the Trettachtal. Or, if you want to try your muscles further, you can climb by way of the Heil-bronnerweg to the Kempter refuge, which is nearly 2,000 metres above sea level.

Around Oberstdorf the mountains loop to form a sort of geographical pocket and, at the bottom of this, you will find the Kleinwalsertal, with the villages of Hirschegg, Riezlern and Mittelberg. This is one part of the Allgäu which does not technically belong to Bavaria. Its inhabitants are Austrians but, because they are almost completely cut off from their mother country by the mountains, they have for a long while been Germans for all practical purposes. Their letters must still carry Austrian stamps, although they use German currency!

The Kleinwalsertal takes its name from some remarkable people called the Walsers. Nearly 1,000 years ago, after the complete collapse of the Roman empire, these folk marched north looking for a new land in which to live. Some of them settled in Switzerland – the Canton of Wallis (Valais) is called after them – and others pressed on over the mountains to occupy what is now known as Liechtenstein. The remainder, not more than a hundred in all, crossed the valley of the Ill in the Vorarlberg and landed up in this tiny part that is half-Bavarian, half-Austrian.

A similar anomaly exists with regard to the border village of Jungholz, which lies north-east of Oberstdorf and about 25 kilometres west of Füssen. Here again the inhabitants are Austrian by nationality – and never cease to remind you of the fact – but are incorporated with the Germans.

This area, incidentally, is absolutely perfect for a simple winter sports holiday. Jungholz has a good ski school for beginners. Unterjoch, not far away, also has a school and an elementary ski jump. Hindelang, a little further south, is probably one of the best places of all in which to learn the art of ski-jumping and, back in the Kleinwalsertal, the villages are literally seething with eager young instructors, whilst you will find more than a dozen ski lifts, three chair lifts and even a cable railway, together with three ski jumps, all in the space of a few square kilometres!

At the same time, it must be remembered that all of these places are, like Oberstdorf, not to be ignored during the summer months. My so-called geographical pocket happens to be a re-

22 *Hohenschwangau: the castle and the Alpsee*

markable sun-trap and the warm air caused by long hours of sunshine is held firmly in place by the mountain walls, only gently moved from time to time by the cool, balmy breezes coming down the valleys. You will depart from a holiday here feeling fitter than you have ever felt before and my guess is that you will be back the following year.

If you don't possess a car and enjoy walking, I have a suggestion to make. Take a train from Immenstadt to Oberstdorf, stay there for a night or two, then walk slowly back down the valley, taking a good look at all the villages you pass en route and stopping the night at cheap little *Gasthäuser*. I spent a week doing this not many years ago and it did me a power of good. It also taught me more about this part of the Allgäu than I could have learnt from all the guidebooks ever published.

23 *Neuschwanstein*

11. Envoi

A composer faced with the task of concluding a noble symphony usually takes all the instruments of the orchestra and scores for them a great crescendo, reprising his main theme and ending with a series of majestic, crashing chords. I cannot do that with this slight, all too inadequate symphony of Bavaria. I am forced to finish on something of an anticlimax, a diminuendo that, whilst holding a faint echo of former splendours, leads into nothing more than one final scintillating arpeggio.

Had I stopped this book amid the medieval grandeur of Bamberg or Regensburg, in the great art galleries of Munich or even amongst the beautiful mountain regions of the Allgäu, I would have had my triumphal ending ready-made. But I have chosen to make a very nearly circular tour of Bavaria and, as I approach my starting point, the line I have inscribed becomes less marked.

After Immenstadt and nearby Bühl am Alpsee, with its attractive little lake, the road to the border undulates through largely agricultural country, mostly at a level of 800 metres, until it reaches Oberstaufen. Here you will find two smallish Gothic churches in the vicinity, but there is little else of architectural or historical note and, if you are making the journey during the summer, the surroundings may depress you. Oberstaufen and the adjoining small town of Steibis, three kilometres away, don't really come to life until mid-winter, when they are immensely popular with skiers aiming to become experts, most of them arriving from the Lake Constance area just for the day or for the weekend.

And now the main road out of Bavaria starts to descend from the plateau, only to rise again sharply as it approaches Schneidegg, the Free State's most westerly winter sports resort at the extreme limit of the Allgäu Alps, which stands at a height of 900 metres. From here you must descend steeply again until you reach the eastern end of Lake Constance, some 500 metres below.

The Bavarian border actually touches about 15 kilometres of the lakeside, from just to the west of Nonnenhorn to just below the town of Lindau. The former is little more than a village, but it is a delightful place to frequent on a warm summer's day, when you can eat and drink in its attractive Seegarten right on the water's edge. Between it and the Lindau are Wasserburg, built with its small church on a little peninsula, Enzisweiler and Bad Schagen, where you could find yourself spending a lot of money if you wished to take the cure! It is in fact a favourite resort of wealthy industrialists from Frankfurt and the Ruhr area and not really to be visited by the mere English tourist.

Lindau, also, is an expensive place in which to stay, but it is well worthy of a brief visit. The old town, formerly an imperial free city, is built on an island in the lake and seen from above it looks rather like a giant raft attached to the mainland by slender gangways, which are its two bridges about a kilometre apart. You must be extremely cautious when you drive across the main bridge, because the police are always there watching the traffic like hawks and, I regret to say, they are not too well endowed with either a sense of humour or a feeling of compassion for indiscreet foreign tourists. Only a few years ago, I found myself involved in a snarl-up concerning rights of way on the shore side of this bridge, with a dozen infuriated, red-faced policemen blowing whistles continuously when they were not jotting down the names of alleged offenders in their little books. My rage at being screamed at by one of these uniformed oafs largely subsided when I was informed by a little local lady : 'They are not Bavarians, you know. They are Germans.'

The main street of the old town has some delightful burghers' houses with covered balconies, and the remains of its ancient fortifications faintly reprise the main theme of all those medieval towns we have seen through our journey in historic Bavaria. There are three fairly well-preserved towers, the Diebsturm (Thieves' Tower) in which criminals were once incarcerated, and the Pulverturm (Powder Tower) which formed a part of the arsenal, these two being all that are left of the dozen or so encircling the original city, and the thirteenth-century Mangturm, once the lighthouse marking the entrance to Lindau's harbour. This harbour was of great importance during the Middle Ages. It was used by large sailing craft bringing foodstuffs from the great agricultural region at the west end of the lake and by barges transporting royalty and noblemen from the imperial cities of Konstanz and Überlingen.

It must be remembered in this connection that Lake Constance actually forms a part of the river Rhine, which enters it on the Swiss-Austrian border, and Lindau was once held to be a Rhine port, although the river is not fully navigable between the west end of the lake and Bâle.

St Peter's Church, founded at the beginning of the eleventh century, is unique in that it possesses the only wall painting by Hans Holbein the Elder still in existence. And you should also take a look at the Old Town Hall, which was built in 1422-36 and renovated from time to time thereafter. Spare a few minutes, too, for Lindau's interesting little museum, which is housed in the Cawazzen, a patrician house dating back to 1729.

Above all, Lindau is a gay town at all times of the year; some people consider it to be the gayest in all Bavaria. Its narrow shopping streets are always thronged with happy, smiling folk of many different nations from sunrise to sunset, blissfully spending the currencies of Austria, Germany and Switzerland when the light of a myriad coloured lamps are reflected in the waters surrounding the island, Lindau is at its best, with galas without having to resort to money exchanges. And at night, on the lake and orchestras in the restaurants.

Away to the south just before dusk, you will see the pink rays of the setting sun kissing the peaks of the Drei Schwestern, the mountains that stand guard over the little Principality of Liechenstein, 40 kilometres away. And to the west the still, almost motionless waters of Lake Constance stretch beyond eye's reach and blend with the soft music of violins playing the lilting melodies of Strauss.

It is the final arpeggio. A fitting end to a symphony of words that I can only hope you have enjoyed reading as much as I have enjoyed writing.

Index